How
Life Insurance
Companies
Rob You
And
What You
Can Do
About It

How Life Insurance Companies Rob You
And What You Can Do About It

Walter S. Kenton, Jr., CLU

Random House
New York

Library of Congress Cataloging in Publication Data
Kenton, Walter S., Jr., 1942-
How life insurance companies rob you and what you
can do about it.
1. Insurance, Life—United States. I. Title.
HG8951.K4 1982   368.3'2   82-40235
ISBN 0-394-51197-2

Manufactured in the United States of America
9 8 7 6 5 4 3 2
First Edition

To Cathy

Thanks to Booton Herndon and his assistant, Susan Tyler Hitchcock, for the research and presentation of the material in this book.

And a special note of appreciation to our editor, Robert D. Loomis, for his extra and gracious efforts in our behalf.

Contents

How
Life Insurance
Companies
Rob You
And
What You
Can Do
About It

Chapter 1

No One to Turn To

As a responsible person with people dependent upon you, you have a serious problem.

You want to provide for your wife—or husband—and your children if you should be one of the thousands of people your age who will die tomorrow. Unless you're rich, the only way you can do it is with insurance.

And I can tell you from seventeen years of professional experience that if you want sincere and intelligent advice about insurance, you have no one to turn to.

Your lawyer? your accountant? your banker? They can't keep up with the complexities of life insurance and they don't try. Most of the ones I know are paying too much themselves.

Your father? your Uncle Harry? They are paying for policies issued before 1966—based on the mortality rate of the 1800s, including the Civil War.

Your government? By act of Congress, the federal government can't even study the insurance industry, much less regulate it or give you advice about it. There's more control over producing a jelly bean than there is over a million-dollar insurance policy.

Your life insurance agent? That's the biggest joke of all. I was one. The insurance industry has sent me out to sell life insurance to poor families in wretched houses, to multimillionaires in exclusive clubs. I am a Chartered Life Underwriter; I made the Million Dollar Round Table. I won trips to Hawaii and Acapulco. Among my company's 20,000 agents, I was in the top 1 percent. When I switched companies I practically wrote my own ticket. In short, I was successful.

And I was successful not because I sold the life insurance that was best for you, but because I sold the life insurance that was best for *me*.

I didn't realize it myself for a long time. What I really wanted to be as a youth was an Episcopalian minister. I was so brainwashed by the insurance industry that I honestly believed I was devoting my life to helping my fellow-man.

There are 300,000 other life insurance salesmen out there, and I speak for them, too. As a manager I hired, fired, trained, and rode herd on salesmen. I know the pressures put on them to sell. Many can't take it. There's a bigger turnover in life insurance agents than there is in coal miners. The ones who stay are the ones who sell what their companies tell them to sell: the most expensive products.

You think you're providing for your wife and children when you buy insurance. But the person you're really providing for is the salesman and his company.

The livelihood of the life insurance salesman comes from commissions based primarily on the first year's premium. What percentage of that premium do you think we get?

While you're thinking I'll tell you about one of my sales. In recent years I dealt almost exclusively with wealthy people. The challenge is greater and the rewards higher. I had a client who had built his own multimillion-dollar business. I spent a lot of time and energy on him.

First I had to find him; a good proportion of my working time was devoted to looking for people with money. Then I had to meet him, then cultivate him. This man was an outdoors nut. To gain his friendship I joined his hunting and fishing clubs. I went to dull meetings. I helped put on a game dinner. Bear meat. Elephant meat. Ugh. I even went hunting with him. I hated it, but the client thought I was a great guy. He trusted me.

I suggested an analysis of his estate—you don't think I told him I was a life insurance salesman, do you? The analysis showed his holdings to be so big that on his death it would take $1 million to pay taxes, legal fees, and other expenses.

"My God, what'll I do?" he asked.

That's when I suggested life insurance.

Of course, he was grateful.

I had a $1 million policy tailored especially for him. I selected it from the three following possibilities:

1. Permanent, or whole life, insurance with the company I represented, annual premium $47,000.

2. Term insurance with my company, initial annual premium $25,000.

3. Term insurance with a more competitive company, initial annual premium $18,000.

I'll explain about term and permanent insurance later. Right now all that matters is that each one of those policies pays $1 million, no more, no less, when he dies.

So which policy did I present? Any insurance agent could tell you in a second. If I explain the commission on each policy, you'll know, too.

First, eliminate the low-cost policy from another company. It would have paid a 25 percent commission on the first year premium of $18,000, or $4,500, and my company would have thrown me out on my ear for selling it.

Now let's look at my company's term policy, annual premium $25,000. That would also bring a 25 percent commission, or $6,250.

And finally, the permanent insurance, annual premium $47,000. It costs nearly three times the low-cost policy, though it still pays the same $1 million death benefit. And the commission would be 55 percent of the first year's premium, $25,850, plus extras and bonuses. (It worked out to about $35,000, plus a trip to Hawaii for two.) And I would also receive an appreciable commission on the future annual premiums of $47,000.

So that's what I presented to my client, and that's what I sold. I doubt if he is aware to this day that he could have bought the same amount of insurance for a lot less.

Nor is he aware that he didn't need the insurance in the first place. Estate-tax insurance is a gimmick dreamed up by the life insurance industry for suckers. This man will leave his heirs several million dollars—let them pay the taxes. At that time (prior to the 1981 tax law) they would have had a period of fifteen years in which to pay. That's a hardship? But I was trained not to bring up that provision of the law.

I don't think my client is getting a thing for the $47,000 he puts up every year. I'll tell you who benefits from estate-tax insurance: the insurance company and me. Given his life expectancy and the time value of money, the company stands to take in a lot more than a million by the time they give it back.

Were you surprised to see that a life insurance salesman gets 55 percent commission? Well, let me tell you this: A lot of us get much more than that. Fifty-five percent is the maximum permitted to companies licensed in the state of New York. Many companies deliberately do not do business in New York in order to be able to offer salesmen higher commissions.

When I retired as a full-time insurance agent in order to write this book, I was associated with one of those companies. What commission do you think I got for every permanent, high-cost insurance policy I sold? (I didn't sell any other kind.) Sixty percent? Seventy? *Would you believe 102?* It broke down this way:

Basic commission	60 percent
Expense allowance	18 percent
Performance ($1 million a year)	12 percent
Persistence	12 percent
	102 percent

That's still not tops. You can win bets with this one: A new type of policy called deposit insurance pays the salesman as much as 250 percent of the first year's premium.

According to industry estimates it costs an insurance company an average of 142 percent of the first year's premium to sell any new policy. What this proves is that insurance is so profitable that the companies are willing to spend almost one and a half times your first premium just to get you started making payments.

You don't have to be a millionaire to attract life insurance salesmen. We can do well selling smaller policies—provided they are high-cost insurance. That's why you can't trust your best friend if he's a life insurance salesman. The pressure is on him to sell you *expensive* insurance.

And that's why in this book I refer not to life insurance *agents,* but to life insurance *salesmen.* A true agent represents *you.* He has your interests at heart. Under that definition there is no such thing as a life insurance *agent.* He is a salesman, selling the product his company gives him to sell, with enormous incentives for selling you a high-priced policy.

He may even show you his own. All salesmen are urged to take out an expensive policy on themselves to impress clients with. But we don't tell you that we get it the first year for 60 percent, even 100 percent, off, and after that we let it lapse. What we show you with such assurance isn't worth two cents—except as a sales tool.

If you still think *your* friend is different, let's put it another way. He gets a greater monetary reward for selling you *less* insurance than you need for a higher price than for insuring you adequately at a lower price.

Here's what I mean. When I first became a life insurance agent, twenty years old with two weeks at training school, I went to my best friend to sell him a policy.

He was my first prospect—and my first rejection.

He was married, he and his wife were both working, and he was going to school at night. He said he didn't need insurance and he got a little huffy with me when I insisted that *everybody* needs insurance.

Two weeks later I heard his wife was pregnant. In training school they taught us that any change in the domestic pattern was an opportunity, and that of all these changes a new baby heads the list. The new father-to-be is all loaded with emotions. He's proud. He's happy. He's aware of his new responsibility—and a little scared of it. I quickly convinced him of his good fortune in having a trained counselor in domestic finance there to help him. (That was me.)

What I was trained in was what the company was pushing at the time—a family policy with everything in it but the kitchen sink. It had a $10,000 permanent, or whole life, policy on himself, a $2,000 policy on his wife, and a $1,000 policy on the child—who wouldn't even be born for eight months. Also double indemnity and paid-up policies for the wife and child in case of his demise.

I stressed the savings feature of the policy, which he needed the way his unborn child needed life insurance, and he bought it completely. The whole package came to $12.50 a month, a pretty stiff obligation for a young man at that time and a pretty good sale for me. I would get 55 percent of the annual premium of $150, or $82.50, plus a big shot in the ego.

Ten days later he was killed in an automobile accident.

Can you imagine my feelings when I personally put into the young widow's hands a check for $20,000, double the face amount for accidental death?

In training school we all had memorized a question: Could you face the widow of your best friend and confess you neglected to provide him with insurance?

Now here was the proof of everything they had taught me. Insurance was *good.* I was almost happy. We cried together as she held the check.

Later on she wrote me a little note, very sincere and appealing, and I had it encased in plastic along with a clipping of his death and a photostat of the check. It was a marvelous sales tool. It helped me sell millions of dollars' worth of insurance for thousands of dollars' worth of commissions.

My friend's wife went back to her family and I never saw her again. I wonder how long the $20,000 lasted. She probably spent some of it to get her through the delivery and the following months. Even if she managed to keep it intact and invested it wisely, it wouldn't have brought her more than $1,000 to $1,200 a year.

For that $150 annual premium, instead of the Mickey Mouse policy I sold him, he could have bought $50,000 worth of term insurance with a double indemnity clause. That would have given her $100,000, which at the time would have provided an income of $5,000 or $6,000 a year, plus Social Security, and, of course, a great deal more today.

But my commission would have been only $37.50. I never even thought of it.

Chapter 2

Ravenous Wolves

Beware of false prophets, which come to you
in sheep's clothing, but inwardly they are
ravening wolves.

MATTHEW 7:15

Don't judge me too harshly. Maybe selling too little insurance at too high a price was reprehensible, but I was so brainwashed by the insurance industry that it took me seventeen years to realize it. I was trained to sell my company's product. If I had tried to provide my friend with more insurance at a lower cost, which is what he needed, all my superiors right up to those in the national office would have had a fit. The other salesmen would have looked at me with amusement or contempt. I'd have done no good for anyone, most of all me. Because I'd have been out of the insurance business almost before I was in it.

I'm going to talk a lot about life insurance salesmen, sales techniques, and industry marketing in this book. As far as I know, it's a first. I've never heard of or read about any life insurance salesman who told the public the truth about selling life insurance.

Why should you care? Because this industry is enormous

and it's completely uncontrolled. Someday somebody has got to do something about it. Right now nobody outside the business knows enough to begin. It appears to be a big, highly visible industry with TV ads, skyscrapers, and agents who are church deacons and Rotary presidents. There is just no public comprehension of this business except for a very few academic experts who make it even more complicated than it is and confuse more than they explain.

I don't pretend to be an insurance industry analyst, but I do know one thing: This entire enormity is based on marketing, and marketing is based on the individual salesman.

Understanding the salesman is the place to begin.

I'm assuming you need or think you need insurance, or are concerned about somebody close to you who needs insurance, or you're going to be the beneficiary of somebody who needs insurance. You also may need good low-cost insurance to replace inadequate, high-cost insurance. In order to get the insurance you need, unless you're one of a few exceptions, you're going to have to deal directly with one or more life insurance salesmen and indirectly with one or more life insurance companies.

These people are trained to sell their products. They are competitors in a dog-eat-dog world. They are not only out to get your money, but to beat you at their game.

When I was a life insurance salesman, I was one of an army of people doing things for you. Service clubs couldn't run without us. We're active in church work, charitable drives, community functions of all kinds. I held every office in my local Jaycee chapter up to the presidency. That meant many, many hours of work, which could be paid for only by selling my fellow members and other contacts high-cost insurance. I could hardly put in Jaycee time and direct selling time on the insurance young men in that age group really needed, in the amount they could pay for. If you're a Jaycee with insurance bought from another Jaycee, you're paying his dues.

When I moved to a new town I was too old for the Jaycees so I joined the Kiwanis. By volunteering, extending myself, I was named membership chairman—good exposure. The commission on just one sale made it all worthwhile—to me. But the person who bought that policy paid for all my Kiwanis time and the time necessary to work up his policy. It was expensive insurance.

We make it our business to meet people, talk to people, gain their confidence, advise them in many areas that only touch on insurance. The advice is lousy because we slant everything we say.

A life insurance salesman hardly has the time or the background to qualify as a financial consultant in the first place. In the second place, we're prejudiced. I remember reading in some life insurance publication that mutual funds were poor investments, and that is what I have passed on, seriously, authoritatively, to hundreds of clients. Many bought life insurance from me as a result; many more were influenced against mutual funds. It came as a shock to me, after I left the insurance business, to learn that some mutual funds have provided dramatic returns. I wonder how much my advice has cost my clients.

When I went into estate-tax insurance almost exclusively, I set out to cultivate all the important attorneys and trust officers in town. They would provide leads to wealthy clients; I would refer those clients back to them for legal work and trusteeship. Most of the lawyers just really didn't understand the complexities of the estate-tax laws and were quite happy to draw up whatever proposal I submitted. If any of them did see the flaws in buying expensive insurance to pay estate taxes with, they properly, in my opinion at that time, did not so advise their clients.

The one lawyer who advised his clients not to accept the elaborate and costly program I had drawn up for them never got any more business out of me. I took my clients to someone else. But if ever I need legal work, that lawyer is the one I'm going to consult.

If your lawyer or certified public accountant approves of an action on your part in which a permanent insurance policy is involved, suggest to him that he read this book.

I could give in great detail the complicated explanations and advice of the consumer-oriented organizations, like Consumers Union and the American Institute for Economic Research, but I honestly don't think they would do you one bit of good. They make a comparatively simple concept, getting money for dying, as complicated as advanced economics.

Even if you understand what they're saying, you still have to face that predatory agent with his bag of tricks. He may not be any smarter than you, but he is schooled in selling. I always felt myself more than a match for any client, be he lawyer, accountant, or economist.

Insurance may be the most important purchase of your life, especially if you're wiped out by a drunken driver tonight, as somebody will be. I'm not going to mince words about death or dying in this book. Insurance is money when you're dead. If you're not going to die, you don't need insurance or this book. Later on I'm going to show you the mortality tables on which life insurance is based, and you will see just how many people your age are going to die this year.

For all its importance, there's no product or commodity about which the people who buy it know less. They know more about their stereo systems, the cars they drive, or the whiskey they drink than they do about their life insurance policies. They have too much or too little. They have the wrong kind, for the wrong purpose.

And the people who benefit from the life insurance payments, the widows and children, the very people who should know the most about life insurance, know even less than the policyholders. If you are a wife with children, the time for you to know about insurance is *now*.

I know a man who hasn't earned a nickel in thirty-five

years. He's always got great plans and he works hard at them, but they always go wrong. His wife, who's loaded, bails him out. But *he's* the one who has the big, expensive, ego-building life insurance policy, which she pays the premium on.

Another man has so many insurance policies he won't tell me the number. He has put a lot of property in his wife's name, and his children, who are either well married or well employed, are going to inherit plenty. Why is he still paying through the nose for these insurance policies? He's already put in twice what he's going to get out, considering the time value of money, and he keeps shelling out more. I think he just can't stand the idea of dying and not getting something for it.

I know two children, ages two and four, who have big life insurance policies. Who is the beneficiary? The same person who pays the premiums: their wealthy grandmother. They have no income to insure; if they did it wouldn't go to her; she doesn't need the death benefit. It makes no sense at all —except to the salesman who got the commissions.

The industry trains us and equips us for almost every eventuality. One evening I was trying to sell a man a program to provide for his wife and children, but I wasn't getting to first base. So, as I was taught, I began ticking off the other kinds of insurance. No response until I got to endowment insurance. This would pay him a lump sum of money at age sixty-five. His eyes lit up.

So did mine. Now I understood him. He didn't give a damn about his wife and kids. He wanted money for himself. Back into the briefcase went the ordinary life insurance material. Out came the endowment material, which the boys in the marketing department had thoughtfully provided in case just such a situation came up. The company got a nice annual premium, I got a nice fat commission, and the client got what was coming to him, a lousy investment. All in the finest tradition of American business, marketing a product.

But let's not have any illusions that the industry, the company, or the salesman had that guy's interest at heart.

We have very few of our clients' interests at heart. Did any salesman, for example, ever mention to you disability insurance? I'm not talking about the accident and health offers that come in the mail and promise to pay $13 a day for a $200 hospital room if you get hit by a westbound truck on a north–south street. I'm talking about *disability*, the state of being incapacitated by accident or disease so that you cannot work and support your family, but must instead be supported by them. This is worse than death; this is living death.

Disability insurance is available. You can buy it. I recommend it and will discuss it later. But you're going to have trouble buying it from your friendly life insurance agent because he gets more for selling you life insurance.

By now you should be getting my point. You need life insurance, but the only way you can get it is from a ruthless industry that brainwashes its agents and sends them out to get you.

These are the people you'll have to face to get proper insurance coverage. Good policies at low cost are available. But you've got to know exactly what you want and insist on getting it.

I want to accomplish several things with this book, all designed to help you be properly insured at a reasonable cost.

I want to help you determine how much insurance you need—how much money your dependents need when you're dead. Unless you're very wealthy, you'll never get honest advice from a life insurance salesman on this vital question. But if you work out your own insurance needs according to the formula I will give you, you will be secure and confident in your own mind and you will be able to insist on getting that amount of insurance—or no insurance at all.

When I say "you" in this book I'm usually thinking of the typical person I sold insurance to for seventeen years, the wage earner, the husband, the man. If "you" are a woman, wage earner or homemaker, however, your contribution to your family also has a monetary value. "You" applies to you, too.

Further, because insurance is a death benefit to replace the earnings of the family provider, it is far more important to the beneficiary than to the insured. The beneficiary is the one who's going to have to live on it. So if you're a housewife and don't make a penny outside the home, even if you think what you do is not insurable, you should still have a strong voice in your husband's insurance program. It's for you, not him.

So, whoever you are, I am going to show you how to buy the proper amount of insurance, and what to pay for it.

I will tell you quite simply what kinds of insurance there are, what kind you want, and why. The words permanent, cash value, level payment, whole life, ordinary life, term, annual renewable term, deposit term, participating, non-participating, guaranteed cost, universal, all have clear-cut meanings, easy to understand, and I will explain them.

I will also tell you, right now, that there are more than two thousand life insurance companies doing business in the United States today, and that many of them have many different names for the many kinds of insurance plans. I could never keep up with all those names. Why in the world should you? So let's agree right now not to bother with them. We're going to keep this thing simple.

Suppose you already have a policy. Do you understand it fully? Do you know what it's worth? What is it *really* costing you? What are its features? I'll show you how to analyze it. How does it compare with a competitive policy for a person of your age? (In the insurance business, we don't say low-cost or inexpensive; we say *competitive.*) I have never seen a simple, easy-to-understand, adequate cost comparison of insurance policies before, and I bet you haven't either. Well, I have prepared one. You'll find it in Chapter 10.

Right now, here's a quick experiment. Write down the total of all the payments you will make for life insurance this year. That's Figure A. Write down the amount on the face of your policy. (If you have more than one policy, write down the total.) Divide by 1,000. That's Figure B. Now divide A by B. That's what you are paying for $1,000 worth of insurance.

Even if your policy is only a couple of years old, I'll bet you pay more money for less coverage than what is available to smart shoppers today.

Now look at the premium per thousand for a low-cost $100,000 policy (the 3(T) column) as listed in the table in Chapter 10:

Age 25 — 1.12		Age 45 — 1.75
30 — 1.12		50 — 2.51
35 — 1.17		55 — 3.50
40 — 1.42		60 — 5.31

Depending on when you bought your policy, who sold it to you, and what kind and what value it is, you may be well insured. But it's more likely that you have expensive, antiquated junk, geared to the interest rates of yesterday.

Among the many new developments in the insurance industry are two that you can specifically take advantage of to save money. One is the general reduction in rates that several companies have recently begun offering. Another is the recent acceptance on the part of insurance companies of the medical fact that nonsmokers live longer, and the resulting special reduction for people who don't smoke cigarettes. If you have not smoked for a year since you bought life insurance, you will unquestionably be able to save many times the price of this book on a new nonsmoker's policy.

If you do smoke, quit. In one year to date you'll be able to buy a nonsmoker's policy. You'll also save many times the price of this book, let alone the cost of the cigarettes, and the insurance industry bets its money that you will live longer to spend it!

Smoker or nonsmoker, you will be better off shopping for insurance the way you shop for anything else. I'll show you how to do it.

I have also shown some people how to convert their old policies into a fund that will pay for much better coverage —at no cost to them whatever.

But you will still have to work with a salesman to get the new policy, which is where we started.

Chapter 3

Seventeen Years in the Insurance Business

If you wanted a perfect example of an insurance salesman, you couldn't do better than me.

One of my first memories is having to be quiet when my father came home grumpy from his dull job with the federal government in Washington. I knew I didn't want a routine, nine-to-five job when I grew up.

I also knew I wanted to help people. I wanted people to like me. I learned early that no matter whom I was dealing with, parents, teachers, schoolmates, if I could get people to like me life was easier. I worked hard at it and I received privileges instead of punishment at home, had good friends instead of a bloody nose and skinned knuckles in the neighborhood, and got good grades for less work in the schoolroom. I learned to play a guitar in order to entertain people and I was the leader of a good rock band. I was president of my class in high school and president of the student council. I was offered college scholarships and chose Western Maryland College at Westminster. I wanted to be an Episcopalian minister, but I thought I'd get a general education first.

Instead, I got married. My first wife was two years ahead of me in college and when she graduated she couldn't get a job in Westminster. So we moved to Washington, where she taught school and I was a clerk-typist for the federal government. I still wanted to help people, protect people, so I went to a police academy at night.

We were scratching away when it came time to pay the premium on the insurance policy my father had started for me years ago. I learned that I could cash it in for $300. I called the insurance company and they sent a young man to try to talk me into keeping the policy in force and to sell me more. I insisted on cashing it in, so then he asked me if I'd like to work for the insurance company. What a compliment! (I realize now that he probably got an override for recruiting me.)

The manager gave me an aptitude test. It had questions like, Would you rather read a book or talk to people? It was obvious what they wanted me to answer, so I did. The manager was very pleased. He wanted me! He outlined a terrific program. I would get a starting salary of $100 a week.

I would go to New York City for two weeks' training, all expenses paid. Go by train, live in a hotel—I'd never done either. So I bought a new suit and a gray snap-brim hat and got on the train to New York.

The training course proved I had done the right thing. I quickly realized that life insurance was a higher calling than the ministry and law enforcement combined. Life insurance would take care of your dependents if, God forbid, something should happen. But life insurance was also a living benefit. It would enable you to save money so that, should some dire emergency occur or should you want to make a down payment on a home, it would be right there waiting for you. It was like eating your cake and having it too. Alive or dead, with life insurance, you couldn't lose.

The only catch was that not everybody out in the great wide world appreciated the value of life insurance. Those unfortunates would have to be sold. And so, for the greater part of the two weeks' training period, my fellow trainees learned how to sell life insurance.

Not one step in the sales procedure was left to chance. We practiced knocking on doors. We practiced making our entrance, taking off our hats, and shaking hands. We practiced placing husband and wife together, on my right, so that I could see them both, and so that they could not signal one another.

We learned never, never, never to say "Sign here." People have an aversion to signing things. Rather, we learned to tender the pen with studied casualness, and say, "Would you verify this for me, please?" or "Now I need your name right here."

We learned techniques for making the first contact, for setting up the first appointment. We would never say, for example, "When may I come to see you, sir?" He might say, "Never."

Rather, we would say, "Now, would seven o'clock Tuesday evening be convenient, or would you prefer eight o'clock Wednesday?"

There were people in my training class old enough to be my father, people who supported wives and children, but no one studied harder, practiced harder, worked harder than I did. I believed. And when I finished up the course on Friday and took the train home carrying my bag and wearing my hat, I couldn't wait until Monday to get started.

I already had my prospects. If there is one thing that is constant in the insurance business, as fixed as the North Star, it is Project One Hundred—a list of one hundred prospects. All companies require it. Under this procedure, the recruit, before he goes on the payroll, before he goes to his first training session, before he buys his hat, must produce a list of one hundred names, complete with vital statistics such as age, occupation, and number of children, as well as estimates of income and net worth. (You've probably been on somebody's list, but did you know it was that detailed?) In his first month the recruit, accompanied by the manager, is going to call on each one of these one hundred prospects to sell him insurance.

On Saturday morning, before I had even been to the office, without even any applications, I set out to see my prospects. I sold three policies over the weekend.

At the age of twenty I was an agent for the Metropolitan Life Insurance Company.

After I exhausted my list of one hundred prospects, not all of whom were delighted to see me, I set out to get more. In order to make my solicitations in the same neighborhood, I rented an address directory from the telephone company for $8 a quarter. My company had several form letters and I chose the one featuring savings: through life insurance you could build up a nest egg for the future. I sent out a hundred a week. My wife addressed the envelopes in longhand, and I followed them up at night by phone, making appointments.

In my first full year with the company, when I was twenty-one, I led all forty agents in the Washington office.

In addition to selling insurance, I had to collect for it. At the time, Metropolitan was very big on what was called monthly debit insurance, the kind you collect. My area included a rural area in Maryland with sharecroppers living in shacks right out of *Tobacco Road*. At least the collection part was easy. The people were terrified of letting their insurance lapse. If they weren't at home, they'd leave their quarters hidden under loose boards on the front stoop.

I remember an enormous woman running after me with her money, shouting, "Don't let my policy co-lapse."

Having a policy was a status thing. Even newborn babies had to have a policy. Once I was sitting on a packing box, filling out an application, when a rat ran through the room.

On Fridays salesmen from different companies lined up at the courthouse to copy down names of people getting marriage licenses. Then we'd hit them over the weekend.

We'd spend several hours a week cold canvassing—knocking on doors. The gimmick was a cookbook. Knock knock, lady comes to door, try to get her to take a cookbook. Sometimes it was an interesting contest. I'd shove it at her, almost poke her in the nose with it, as she'd squirm and dodge to keep from taking it. Because she knew that once she took it she was obligated.

All the time I was talking. "Hello there. I'm Walt Kenton, Metropolitan Life. Just thought I'd drop around and see the people in the neighborhood today. You know, Metropolitan is just down the road here [more like ten miles]. This is certainly a nice house. What does your husband do? By the way, who do you have insurance with? Oh, I know you're not in the market for insurance. After all, I'm just dropping by like a neighbor. But let me show you something that might be of interest sometime in the future [now I'd pull out another piece of literature, like a Social Security Estimator]. This is a free service, no obligation except to those you love. [*No obligation except to those you love.* We had to memorize that, and I've said it so many times they ought to put it on my tombstone.] How much would Social Security pay you if something terrible happened to your husband tomorrow? I *thought* you wouldn't know. Now you see how valuable this service will be for you? Would you like me to explain it further? Let's see, I can come by Wednesday night at seven o'clock, or would Thursday at eight o'clock be more convenient?"

You can't believe what women will tell you at the front door. They'd ask me in for a cup of coffee and tell me the damnedest personal gossip, and I knew that I was going to come back some evening and maybe make a sale.

This sounds like the pits, and it was. But it was also good training. After a few years of knocking on thousands of doors in two-bit trailer parks or low-cost housing developments, approaching a multimillionaire in the sauna of my club was easy. In all situations I carried with me a magic spell, given to all new agents in those training sessions. It was beaten into us:

We were taught to assume consent.

You can't realize what a powerful weapon this is unless it is a part of your own experience. We were taught, and I believed, that every husband and father should have life insurance. He should work, go to church, place his hand over his heart when the flag went by, and have life insurance. When I offered him life insurance, therefore, he would consent and be grateful.

Believing this, I could approach anyone. This assumption was like a guardian angel hovering over every interview. Suppose, for example, someone told me, "I can't afford life insurance."

Well, I just simply didn't believe it. Life insurance is so important that *everybody* can afford it. What he must have meant was that he was spending money for golf, or beer, or medical bills, or some other frivolity. Secure in my assumption that he really wanted and needed life insurance, I would press on. We had an arsenal of gimmicks, sales tools furnished by the company. I've known agents who actually carried a miniature hearse with them (you can buy them) and pulled it out at the right moment.

Suppose you looked me in the eye and said, "I wouldn't buy insurance from you because you're a no 'count son of a bitch."

I would answer, "I'm sure you must have some reason for your opinion, but surely a perceptive individual like you wouldn't let that interfere with finding a solution to your problems."

"But I don't have any problems, goddamnit!"

"I'm sure you don't," I would say. "And if we could sit down quietly together I could provide you with some information that will be of great help to you in continuing that enviable condition."

I never disagreed with anybody. You say you're buying insurance from your father?

"Well, I certainly approve of maintaining close family ties, but in case you don't want your father to know everything you do, every nickel you make and spend, I would be glad to advise you confidentially and impersonally, as a Chartered Life Underwriter, in your general age group."

You say you are buying your insurance through some group?

"Well, that's a good way to buy your basic insurance policy, yes sir. Of course there may be a time when you need someone close at hand, your personal agent, who cares about you and your wife and your children and your family and can advise you personally and in depth on life insurance—which could be, I certainly hope not but it could be, the most important purchase of your life. And what if you change jobs and are uninsurable?"

You say you have all the insurance you need?

"I'm sure you are quite well insured. As a matter of fact, it's a pleasure to work with people who have demonstrated that they appreciate the importance of insurance in their planning. I'd be glad to take a look at your policies. There's no obligation whatsoever, and I may be able to make some suggestions relative to some progressive new programs the industry has come up with lately."

You say my proposal costs too much and you think you can get it for less?

"I'm sure you probably could. But inasmuch as there are more than two thousand insurance companies, you might spend years shopping around. And I'm sure that you would find our policy to be competitive with any company. More important, I'd like to think that my personal services, the fact that you can come to me at any time and I'll be glad to work with you, would have some value."

You say you can't afford $1,200 a year?

"That certainly does sound like a lot of money, doesn't it? But look at it this way—that's only a hundred dollars a month. Divide that by thirty days, and we get three dollars and thirty-three cents—why, that's only fourteen cents an hour! Surely, sir, you can save fourteen cents an hour for an investment in your future!"

You get the point. Whatever you say, I'll agree with, just as I was taught to do. Then I'll get back to the subject of selling insurance. What you think is a good way of getting rid of me may not bother me at all. If you say you already have insurance, I see that as an invitation to buy more.

(How can you chase the persistent salesman from your door? Two easy ways. The most effective is to say you just don't give a damn about your financial obligations to your wife and children. Let 'em take care of themselves.

(If you don't want to appear to be so selfish, here's another. "I'd be delighted to hear your recommendations, and will pass them on to my regular agent when we get together for our annual review of my policies.")

I liked a short simple comment we were taught in training school. After setting up the dire situation of the husband dying uninsured and the wife having to go to work, I would shake my head sadly and say, "I would hate for the children to lose their mother, *too*." That's a killer.

How much would the insurance cost? Ah, here again, we have powerful tools to work with. We let the family name their own figures—how much it will cost to bury the poor unfortunate, how much it will cost to send his children to Harvard Medical School.

After we established the necessity of income after the husband's imminent death, I would lean forward, look into his eyes, and say, "How much can you save?"

This is a magical phrase. Not "How much can you *pay*?" That would have no impact. Now the responsibility was on him. With his wife and his best friend, his insurance advisor, watching him, his almost-orphan children in the next room, it was up to him to determine how much he could save per month to protect his wife and children. When he came up with a figure, whether it was a dollar or ten dollars, I had him. Now for the coup de grâce:

"Do you wish to name your wife as beneficiary?"

"Shall I schedule your physical examination for Wednesday morning, or would you prefer Friday afternoon?"

At the ripe old age of twenty-two I began to be approached by other companies with interesting offers. The district sales manager heard I was thinking of leaving. The next thing I knew, I was a manager myself. It was flattering at the time, but I realize now that turnover in the life insurance industry is so high that disgruntled salesmen are often made managers, just so they'll stay.

If you knew what a sales manager has to do to hire and train recruits, you would wonder how this industry has managed to sell the five trillion dollars of insurance in force today. I advertised in the Help Wanted columns for salesmen, but it didn't take me long to learn that if I mentioned life insurance, I'd get no calls. My most successful ads were for Management Trainees, although there is no such thing in the insurance business. We used a special telephone number, and that number was never answered with the word "insurance." I kept standing orders with employment agencies, again with instructions not to mention insurance.

Whenever I saw any reasonably presentable male, I'd try to recruit him. Many a poor devil has sold me a shirt, and the next thing he knew he was an insurance salesman. We had to keep pulling them in because we kept losing them.

There are many reasons for the rapid turnover in insurance. The beginning salesman has no prestige in his peer group. His income is low. It's night work, and after the One Hundred names are exhausted, it's tough finding more. Some salesmen are lazy, some are dumb, some are crude, some are unpleasant. Many just can't take it. I recruited two excellent people, a man and his wife. They could not even get through their hundred prospects. They were just simply too nice to be in this game. They were members of my church, and I was embarrassed every time I saw them.

With my religious background, I don't think I ever really did anything dishonest directly, but I knew of a few things. Some years ago, for example, the insurance industry jumped on the bandwagon provided by Congress, which said an employee of an educational institution could invest in tax-sheltered annuities. A teacher could request the school board to withhold a portion of the paycheck to buy them tax free.

What an opportunity! In our area, however, the school board refused to let us come in to make presentations at faculty meetings.

One day the district sales manager sent me to a liquor store to buy a case of Old Grand-Dad. When I got back he gave me some keys and told me to put the booze in the trunk of a car parked behind the building.

The owner of the car was a member of the school board, which subsequently voted by a majority of one to permit us to make our tax-sheltered annuities presentation to the teachers. That deal put at least $10,000 a year in my pocket.

It also proved again just how little most people, even educated people, know about money management. Those teachers snapped up the annuities like hot cakes. There are two reasons why they were terrible investments. One, if the schoolteachers did not keep up with their payments, they might lose most of what they had put in. Two, they received a very low rate of return.

Although by the time I was twenty-six I was Mister Success with $35,000 a year, two cars, and a trip to Hawaii, I'd had enough of the district sales manager. He was dishonest, vicious, and obscene—and that's when he was sober. I tried to get him out of a bar one night and he knocked me cold.

Eight stitches. I quietly gave my résumé to an insurance industry placement bureau.

If I hadn't realized the mediocrity of management in the insurance industry before, I sure learned it then. I got offers from thirty, thirty-five companies. All over the country they were pleading with me to come on board. They flew me to New England, to Chicago, to California. I talked with big companies and little companies, in big cities and small.

It became obvious that I was sought after not just because I was capable, but because so many other managers were not. Some companies were desperate to replace their substandard people, others were frustrated in their desire to expand by the lack of qualified people or even inexperienced people with some indication of potential to manage their new offices.

I could have gone anywhere, but a company I liked offered to open a general agency for me in Washington, D.C., and I accepted. It was the Protective Life Insurance Company of Birmingham, and nobody, including me, had ever heard of it before. But that doesn't matter in the insurance industry. Actually the name on the door was Walter S. Kenton Associates, Financial Planners, and only after you had bought your policy would you have learned, if you bothered to look, the name of the insurance company. Within a couple of months I had a staff of seven, including three retired colonels.

And in two years I was right back with Metropolitan. The regional manager had found out who had been doing the drunken manager's work (me), fired him, and asked me to come back. My wife and I were breaking up; I could go anywhere I wanted. I chose Charlottesville, Virginia, a pleasant community with money falling out of the trees.

For years I had been taking the courses leading to Chartered Life Underwriter, the Ph.D. of the insurance business. The final course is estate planning; I was taking it and teaching it to my staff at the same time. I realized that estate planning was for me. I had the expertise, and the community had the millionaires. No longer would I have to drive twenty miles at nine o'clock at night to sell some reluctant slob a $10,000 policy. I would associate with lawyers, certified public accountants, and trust officers. I would work only days. I would be an estate planner.

It wasn't long before I had to turn in my Corvette and lease a Cadillac in order to keep up with my clients. Without getting up in the morning, I was drawing $20,000 a year on commissions from previous policies. But as a hangover from the old days when agents collected cash, twice a week I had to get to the office at eight-thirty in the morning and hand in a slip marked NIL, for no cash deposited.

I don't think that's worth $20,000 a year, do you? I quit.

This time, with a pretty new blond wife who also enjoyed the finer things in life, it was a most rewarding experience being wined and dined by prospective sponsors. My palate was more sophisticated. I appreciated the Chateaubriand, the rich red aged Bordeaux. I finally decided to go with Integon Life Insurance Company of Winston-Salem, North Carolina, with a commission of 102 percent. As a general agent, I also represented other companies for special types of insurance.

As an estate analyst, I had the unusual opportunity to study the insurance programs people already had. Though my prospects were intelligent enough to have estates worth at least $1 million, I was constantly amazed at how little they knew about their own insurance.

What they had was what the agent sold them. He could have been dumb, or lazy, or greedy. Whatever he was, that's what they got.

I once cultivated a wealthy couple in the hope of selling a big policy to cover their inheritance taxes. They told me they had a policy. I asked to see it.

They pulled out all their documents and for a second there my eyes bugged out. They didn't have one policy—they had *two*. One for $250,000, one for $500,000. I knew what had happened. When agents get word back from the doctor that the prospect passed the medical examination, we prepare an extra policy for a larger amount, just in case.

"Congratulations!" I say, displaying the medical report. "You've passed your physical. Our doctor says you're in such excellent health that we can increase the amount of coverage!"

They grab the larger policy as if it were a prize they'd won.

In this case the agent had prepared two policies, one for the $250,000 agreed upon, and one for $500,000 just in case. Somehow the client had signed *both*. He'd bought three times more insurance than he had originally agreed to buy and he didn't even know it. (The premiums were automatically deducted from his bank account, and apparently he never checked.)

That lucky salesman. He had started out with a sale of $250,000, premium $7,000, of which 55 percent commission would be $3,850. And then he sat there and watched the client sign two policies for a total premium of about $20,000 —$11,000 commission.

From the age of twenty to thirty-eight, I had a rich and varied experience in the insurance industry, as sales representative, sales manager, general agent, and broker, representing companies from the second largest in the world down to companies you never heard of. I studied the operations of a score or more additional companies, from north to south and from east to west. And all this time I kept up with the trade press, the publications of all the satellite organizations of the industry, textbooks and papers of the educational institutions of the industry. I attended—and conducted— more lectures and seminars and training courses than I could possibly count.

I'm sure there must be other experienced, successful insurance salesmen who went into this with the finest of motives and who have since realized how much they were brainwashed, that they are not serving their clients but preying on them. But they have worked themselves up to good incomes, with wives and children dependent on them—and they're trapped. They can't quit. They've got to keep on with this shoddy lifestyle, burying their better instincts, keeping the truth to themselves, putting up a big front with other agents at luncheon meetings.

Well, I was fortunate that, when I realized what I was doing, I *could* quit. And I did.

I think I know something about insurance and the insurance industry. Furthermore, I am no longer in it. I can tell you the truth.

Chapter 4

How Life Insurance Works

Since many companies have marketing experts who devise special policies in order to provide their agents with interesting and different products to sell, the industry makes life insurance appear to be very complicated.

Actually it is very simple. It is based on two easy questions: What are your chances of dying this year? And how long are you going to live?

You don't know? Well, *somebody* knows. The actuaries know. They are the people, insurance company employees, who keep score on life and death in America. Their source of information is the Commissioners 1958 Standard Ordinary Mortality Table, which went into effect in 1966.

If you have an insurance policy issued before 1966, it was based on a period in the 1800s, including the Civil War. Honest. You're paying premiums on a time when your life expectancy was forty-one years. If a bullet didn't get you at Bull Run, you'd still have to survive smallpox, malaria, tuberculosis, polio, or other diseases now under control.

You might be better off replacing that policy entirely. I'll show you how to evaluate it in Chapter 12.

The 1958 table is also obsolete, and heavily weighted in favor of the insurance industry. The Society of Actuaries drew up a new table in 1980. It shows that you are going to live longer than the 1958 table says. It reflects a phenomenon of the past few years, which is bringing about a change in longevity comparable to the control of diseases like small-pox, tuberculosis, and malaria. That is the number of people who have quit smoking, or never started.

The 1980 table also recognizes the existence of females. Previous tables dealt exclusively with male mortality. To figure a woman's insurance premiums some companies take the male rate less three years. Thus, a 26-year-old woman pays the same rate as a 23-year-old man. Some companies set the age back *six* years.

However, the new table will not go into effect until 1989. The 1958 table is still in use today, so let's see how it works.

When were you born? Thirty years ago? Forty? Fifty? Whenever it was, that many years ago, according to the Mortality Table, 10 million babies were born and you were one of them.

If you look at the table, you will see that of those 10 million babies, 70,800 died the first year, or 7.08 per thousand. That's the death rate, 7.08. The next year, age 1, there were 9,929,200 babies left, of which 17,475 died, for a death rate of 1.76.

The death rate remained at less than 2 per thousand until you reached the age of 28, at which point there were 9,519,442 of you remaining; 19,324 died, so the death rate was 2.03.

The table takes you through the nineties. At the age of 98 there will be 19,331 of you left, but 12,916 will die that year, for a death rate of 668.15. For the sake of convenience, the table gives you no chance of living past the age of 100; in the

COMMISSIONERS 1958 STANDARD ORDINARY MORTALITY TABLE

Age	Number Living Beginning of Year	Number Dying During the Year	Death Rate per 1,000	Age	Number Living at Beginning of Year	Number Dying During the Year	Death Rate per 1,000
0	10,000,000	70,800	7.08	50	8,762,306	72,902	8.32
1	9,929,200	17,475	1.76	51	8,689,404	79,160	9.11
2	9,911,725	15,066	1.52	52	8,610,244	85,758	9.96
3	9,896,659	14,449	1.46	53	8,524,486	92,832	10.89
4	9,882,210	13,835	1.40	54	8,431,654	100,337	11.90
5	9,868,375	13,322	1.35	55	8,331,317	108,307	13.00
6	9,855,053	12,812	1.30	56	8,223,010	116,849	14.21
7	9,842,241	12,401	1.26	57	8,106,161	125,970	15.54
8	9,829,840	12,091	1.23	58	7,980,191	135,663	17.00
9	9,817,749	11,879	1.21	59	7,844,528	145,830	18.59
10	9,805,870	11,865	1.21	60	7,698,698	156,592	20.34
11	9,794,005	12,047	1.23	61	7,542,106	167,736	22.24
12	9,781,958	12,325	1.26	62	7,374,370	179,271	24.31
13	9,769,633	12,896	1.32	63	7,195,099	191,174	26.57
14	9,756,737	13,562	1.39	64	7,033,925	203,394	29.04
15	9,743,175	14,225	1.46	65	6,800,531	215,917	31.75
16	9,728,950	14,983	1.54	66	6,584,614	228,749	34.74
17	9,713,967	15,737	1.62	67	6,355,865	241,777	38.04
18	9,698,230	16,390	1.69	68	6,114,088	254,835	41.68
19	9,681,840	16,846	1.74	69	5,859,253	267,241	45.61
20	9,664,994	17,300	1.79	70	5,592,012	278,426	49.79
21	9,647,694	17,655	1.83	71	5,313,586	287,731	54.15
22	9,630,039	17,912	1.86	72	5,025,855	294,766	58.65
23	9,612,127	18,167	1.89	73	4,731,089	299,289	63.26
24	9,593,960	18,324	1.91	74	4,431,800	301,894	68.12
25	9,575,636	18,481	1.93	75	4,129,906	303,011	73.37
26	9,557,155	18,732	1.96	76	3,826,895	303,014	79.18
27	9,538,423	18,981	1.99	77	3,523,881	301,997	85.70
28	9,519,442	19,324	2.03	78	3,221,884	299,829	93.06
29	9,500,118	19,760	2.08	79	2,922,055	295,683	101.19
30	9,480,358	20,193	2.13	80	2,626,372	288,848	109.98
31	9,460,165	20,718	2.19	81	2,337,524	278,983	119.35
32	9,439,447	21,239	2.25	82	2,058,541	265,902	129.17
33	9,418,208	21,850	2.32	83	1,792,639	249,858	139.38
34	9,396,358	22,551	2.40	84	1,542,781	231,433	150.01
35	9,373,807	23,528	2.51	85	1,311,348	211,311	161.14
36	9,350,279	24,685	2.64	86	1,100,037	190,108	172.82
37	9,325,594	26,112	2.80	87	909,929	168,455	185.13
38	9,299,482	27,991	3.01	88	741,474	146,997	198.25
39	9,271,491	30,132	3.25	89	594,477	126,303	212.46
40	9,241,359	32,622	3.53	90	468,174	106,809	228.14
41	9,208,737	35,362	3.84	91	361,365	88,813	245.77
42	9,173,375	38,253	4.17	92	272,552	72,480	265.93
43	9,135,122	41,382	4.53	93	200,072	57,881	289.30
44	9,093,740	44,741	4.92	94	142,191	45,026	316.66
45	9,048,999	48,412	5.35	95	97,165	34,128	351.25
46	9,000,587	52,473	5.83	96	63,037	25,250	400.56
47	8,948,114	56,910	6.36	97	37,787	18,456	488.42
48	8,891,204	61,794	6.95	98	19,331	12,916	668.15
49	8,829,410	67,104	7.60	99	6,415	6,415	1,000.00

year following your ninety-ninth birthday, it says, there will be 6,415 of you left of the 10 million, and all 6,415 will die. The death rate will be 1,000 per 1,000, or 100 percent. If you live to be a hundred, your company assumes you're dead and pays off.

Let's say that you are one of the 9,373,807 people who are 35 years old, and you want to leave your wife $1,000 if you die. So you get 100,000 people together, all 35 years old. The table says the death rate is 2.51 per thousand, which means that 251 are going to die. If you each put up $2.51, there'll be $251,000 in the pot, and 251 widows will each get $1,000.

If more than 251 die, the widows get less. If fewer die, there will be money left over and you will get a refund.

Suppose you don't want to run around signing up 100,000 people. In that case you will be glad to know that there are more than two thousand insurance companies to do it for you. Of course, in order to meet expenses such as paying big commissions and salaries and putting up skyscrapers for home offices, they're going to have to charge a little bit more.

Some insurance companies are owned by their policyholders, and are therefore called *mutual companies.* They return some of the profits to some of their policyholders, or owners, in the form of dividends. As these policyholders participate in the earnings, their policies are called *participating,* or par for short.

The other companies are owned by stockholders, as are most corporations, and are called *stock companies.* Some of these companies do issue participating policies that pay dividends, but we usually think of a policy from a stock company as *non-participating,* or non-par. Some companies call it *guaranteed cost.* It costs less initially because you are not going to get any refund or dividend. I have sold both participating and non-participating policies, for both mutual and stock companies, sometimes concurrently.

You already know more than most of the people I sold insurance to, but let's educate you one step further.

When you put up your $2.51 at the age of 35, you were buying insurance for a term of one year. That is what is called *term* insurance.

With term insurance, when the year is finished, so is your policy. For the next year you start all over again. But because the death rate is higher—more people die at 36 than at 35 —you have to pay $2.64. If you keep living and keep buying life insurance, you're going to have to pay a fortune. At the age of 99 you'll pay $1,000 per $1,000.

The insurance industry recognized long ago that you would not want to pay those high premiums in later years. You might not want or need the insurance, either, but the industry didn't even consider that possibility. Rather, it came up with a system of level payments. You pay the same amount of money each year for the same amount of insurance. As you pay until you die, level payment insurance is also known as *permanent* insurance. Of course, the younger you started, the less your annual premium would be. But, in order to average out those heavy payments in later years, it was still a lot more than if you just bought that one-year term.

So a major criticism of level-premium insurance is that you pay more when you're a young fellow and can't afford it, less when you're an old fellow and don't need it.

Suppose you paid on this policy for fifty years and then, just when you were all set to die and hit the jackpot, you couldn't get up the money for the premium. You'd forfeit everything you'd put in. Believe me, it happened. It happened so often that the consumers forced the companies to set aside a portion of the annual premium as a kind of savings account on behalf of the policyholder. This is called non-forfeiture, or cash value. If you stop paying your premiums you do not forfeit your cash value: it will be used until it runs out to keep the insurance in force. If you want to cancel the insurance, you can collect the cash value. Or you can borrow it, at interest, and keep your policy in force.

This kind of insurance has several names: *permanent, cash-value,* and *whole life* are the most common.

Term insurance also has different names. When the company guarantees to renew it each year, it's called *annual renewable term,* ART, or *yearly renewable term,* YRT.

In addition, the company may guarantee to convert it to permanent insurance. Then it's *convertible annual renewable term,* CART.

There are many variations on both term and permanent insurance. Each company has its own trade names for its various products; there are thousands of them. A few permanent policies cost less than some term policies in the early years, but in this book, at least, we consider term low-cost insurance, perm high-cost. I will compare prices in detail later on, but for now, let me give you two figures.

At age 35, in 1982, you could buy a $100,000 term policy from Standard Security Life Insurance Company of New York for $117.

Or you could buy the same amount of permanent insurance from the Fidelity Life Association of Illinois for $2,338.

The protection is the same—$100,000 when you're dead. It's the initial premium that's different—$117 or $2,338. So which would the average consumer buy?

If your answer was $117, you'd better keep on reading this book. It just so happens that the average consumer is not going to buy the $117 policy because he's never going to hear about it in the first place, and if he does, he's going to have trouble finding someone to sell it to him.

Why? Because the commission on the $117 policy is 25 percent—$29.25. The commission on $2,338 is at least 60 percent—$1,403—plus extras. A successful life insurance salesman wouldn't waste time on a $117 policy. I can remember selling only one low-cost policy in my entire career, and that was to get my foot in the door. I went back the following year and talked my client into a nice permanent policy with a 102 percent commission.

Let's look at some of the kinds of permanent insurance you can buy.

Perhaps the most expensive is *endowment.* You pay a specified amount per year for a specified number of years, at which time the company is going to give you a specified amount of money—endow you with it. Between the time you make your first payment and the time you receive your endowment, the company figures it will make, through wise investment and compounded interest, a lot more than the endowment. And, of course, if you die the second after you hand the salesman your check, the company will pay your beneficiary the full amount.

Whether it's you or your beneficiary who collects, the money can be paid in any way that you and the company have agreed on: lump sum, annual payments, monthly payments for a designated time or for as long as you live. This is true of nearly all insurance policies: the payment can be made in a lump sum, over a period of time, or a combination.

Unlike endowment, you have to die to collect on most types of insurance. The next most expensive kind is that which is paid up in a certain number of years. It might be expressed as *Twenty Payment Life, Thirty Payment Life,* or *Paid Up at Sixty, Paid Up at Seventy.* All permanent insurance is paid up at age 100; relax and enjoy it.

All the time I was selling insurance, I never pushed the Paid-Up-at type of policy, because I thought it was dumb. It was such a bad deal that I didn't want to go to the trouble of selling it. Let's say it costs a man $50 a month for $100,000 worth of permanent insurance. To be paid up at 65, he will have to pay $80 a month. For the same $80 another person buying straight life, not Paid Up at 65, can get a $125,000 policy.

When he dies, the man with paid-up insurance leaves his wife $100,000. The other man leaves his wife $125,000.

But they don't die, so at the age of 65, the first man is all paid up. He thinks he has beaten the system. The other man isn't paid up, but he looks on the back of his policy and sees that he can quit paying his premiums and take a reduced policy for, guess what—$100,000! The same thing, and he has had a higher death benefit all those years. And that's what insurance is, death benefit.

I don't recommend either one of those policies. I just wanted to show that the limited-payment policies are even worse buys than straight life policies. They are throwbacks to the original insurance policy—single-payment life. A couple of hundred years ago that was the only insurance there was, and only the wealthy could afford it. Then altruistic (greedy) companies made it possible for more people to buy insurance, by stretching the premium out over a longer period of time. Anyway, in seventeen years I sold just one single-payment policy. The client paid $27,000, as I recall, for $100,000 death benefit.

To show how ruthless insurance marketing can be, let me tell you about a popular insurance plan known as College Life. I didn't sell it, but I know a man who bought it. A few years ago life insurance salesmen swarmed onto college campuses offering seniors a marvelous insurance deal. For simply signing a piece of paper, they would have life insurance coverage for two years without any payment. Only in the third year, when they'd be out in the real world making their fortunes—which was a long way away—would they begin to pay.

These kids didn't need insurance in the first place. Nobody was dependent on them. But the real injustice was that they actually signed a note for an amount equal to the first two years' premiums plus interest. Not to the insurance company, but to a local bank. The premiums were high because the insurance was very expensive and the interest was high. For those able and willing to pay the premiums the third, fourth, and fifth years, the policy would have built up enough cash value to have paid off the note. But by that time most would drop the insurance and lose what value they had. *Then* they learned they had to pay off the note they owed the *bank*. The insurance company, which cooked up the whole sordid mess, was out of it altogether.

Some forms of permanent insurance begin with a lower premium for a few years. Because the payments are reduced, or modified, this type of policy is known as *modified life*. At some point, however, the amount of the annual premium has to be raised sharply beyond the average in order to make up for the lower premiums at the onset.

The industry stresses the savings feature of permanent life insurance, and that's how most agents sell it. But what happens to that savings when a calamity strikes and you've got to put the money for that big insurance premium somewhere else? If you had been making deposits regularly in a savings bank, you can go to the bank and say you're sorry that you not only can't put anything in but must take all you can out.

But let your insurance lapse in the first few years and you've got nothing, or next to nothing. That marvelous savings feature your best friend the insurance salesman told you about has vanished into thin air. Because until you've had the policy a year or two, maybe even more, depending on the company, it has no cash value.

I've had clients with annual premiums as high as $3,000 fail to make the payments the second year. They didn't get back a penny. The person paying $3,000 a year could have bought a term policy for the same amount of insurance for less than $500. So the company wound up with a windfall of $2,500.

I remember a doctor who was paying $227 a month. He ran into some personal difficulties in the second year and could not continue paying. The company lapsed his insurance. Another client in a similar position was a big dairy farmer who was paying about $260 a month on a permanent policy designed to take care of the estate taxes on his death so that the children could inherit the entire operation without selling off the land to pay the tax. Well, the bottom dropped out of the milk business. He came to me for help, and I arranged for him to borrow on the cash value of other policies to pay the premiums. Eventually he ran out of all his cash value. His entire insurance program lapsed.

Both the doctor and the dairy farmer could have maintained their death benefit with term insurance. They could have afforded the low premiums. However, I never even considered mentioning it to them. What I did consider was that they would lose their policies, times would get better, and I'd come back and sell them another expensive policy with another fat commission. If I had gotten mushy and sold those people term insurance, I would have taken myself out of the market for permanent.

Suppose they had died when uninsured and left their survivors nothing? Tough.

The pits of life insurance is known by such dignified terms as industrial, or home service insurance. Fortunately, few readers of this book will be victimized by the companies specializing in it.

Industrial insurance is sold door to door in working-class neighborhoods or ghettos. The agents come around weekly or monthly to collect premiums of a dollar or two. It's very high-cost insurance, designed to soak the ignorant and the poor. If policyholders let it lapse, even after years, they lose everything. But about 200 companies share a take of some $4 billion a year from this shameful business.

I mentioned term insurance briefly before—ART and CART. Let's explore it more fully now.

As I said, term insurance is written for a specific period of time. When the term is ended you are no longer insured. If you have had a heart attack in the meantime, the company probably won't insure you again. Fortunately, many companies provide *renewable term,* which the company guarantees to renew year after year to whatever age it specifies.

A new gimmick in term insurance, one of the few that

benefits the consumer, is *revertible term.* Revertible and renewable insurance is a good deal if you can get it. If you are
in good health and don't smoke when you sign up, you pay
a reduced rate. When you renew the policy, you answer three
questions: Have you seen a doctor or been advised to have
medical treatment or been a patient in a medical institution?
Has any other insurance company turned you down? Are
you now in good health? If the company is satisfied with your
answers, you continue at the same reduced rate structure. If
not, you revert to the company's regular rate. Even if the
company does not like your answer, if you're at death's door,
it still must renew your insurance.

In *convertible term,* the company guarantees that you will
be able to convert it to permanent insurance up to a specified
year. So what? I see no reason to pay extra for a guarantee
to convert to more expensive insurance.

Decreasing term insurance is based on the reasonable assumption that as you grow older you need less insurance.
Sooner or later, for example, your children are going to quit
school and go to work. In decreasing term the premium
remains the same but the amount of insurance decreases so
that you are paying a little for a lot at the beginning, a lot
for a little at the end. It is a comparatively economical, easy
way of buying insurance, and many people do it. However,
I think it is sounder to reassess your insurance program each
year on its merits, and to provide your beneficiaries with
insurance according to current and practical needs, not some
outdated formula. And suppose you are locked into a de-
creasing-term program and you suddenly find yourself with
a new bouncing baby beneficiary.

One type of term insurance to avoid is known in the industry as *deposit term.* This is insurance with what might be a
reasonable premium, but with an additional sum demanded
in advance. It's a good deal for the company, because with
that much deposit up front you have to keep paying. The
deposit itself is working for the company; any amount of

interest you will get on it is a small proportion of the total when the time value of your money is considered.

This is the type of insurance that pays up to 250 percent commission on the first year's premium and is usually marketed by high-pressure salesmen. If you act knowledgeable, and wave this book like an exorcism, they will probably go away.

Group insurance accounts for billions of dollars worth of term insurance in force today. Many corporations, large and small, offer term insurance free or at reasonable rates to their personnel as a fringe benefit. If it's free, you'd be silly not to accept it. However, it might be worth remembering that you can't take it with you if you leave your company.

Group insurance that you pay for is not always a bargain. When I joined Integon, for example, I naturally looked into their group program and found the premiums to be heavily weighted in favor of the older and senior personnel. At my age, it was cheaper to buy an individual policy from another company than from my own group. Insurance for federal government employees is likewise a better buy for the mature employees, which means that it is not so good a buy for the junior personnel. Remember that all group insurance, no matter who makes it available to you, is written by some insurance company according to its own mystical actuarial tables plus greed. Your group may have a lousy deal. No matter what glowing description of the program the brochure may give you, make a cold-blooded comparison of its rate with other rates given in the table in Chapter 10.

You may also encounter *mortgage insurance* and *credit insurance,* issued by your bank or retailer on loans or charge accounts. The premiums appear to be small, but annualized they mount up. These types of insurance are very expensive, and in addition the bank or merchant gets a commission on top of the commission collected by whoever made the contact. Your insurance program should cover your debts anyway, at a much lower price.

Both permanent and term insurance policies come with what the industry calls riders, and what I call frills. These are extras that you pay for, and while each may be only a few dollars a year, it would be wiser to put that money into more insurance, or into something else entirely.

You've heard of double indemnity, for example, or triple indemnity. In spite of the dramatic occasions when it did apply, even when I was a salesman I thought the extra premium was a waste of money and didn't push it. Let's say that you are insured for $50,000; the double indemnity clause provides that if you die in an accident, you'll get $100,000. Surely you can see the fallacy of paying out good money for this kind of thing. Such reasoning defeats the entire purpose of insurance. If your beneficiaries need $100,000 when you die, they need it whether you are killed by a virus or a vehicle. It's like spending money for flight insurance. Why would you need more insurance all of a sudden, just because you are getting on an airplane? If anything, I would need less, because Cathy, my wife, would sue the hell out of the airlines.

The one justification for buying double indemnity is in the case of a young man with a family and low income who does not have the money for the amount of insurance he needs. As a proportion of males that age do die in accidents, he could buy as much term insurance as he can afford, then add double indemnity and hope for the worst.

Another frill is the option to buy additional permanent insurance at specific ages in the future. You're paying for an invitation to the salesman to sell you more expensive insurance when option time comes. You can bet he has marked it on his calendar.

Another waste of money is the rider that provides for the waiver of premiums in case you are disabled. Sure, that sounds good, particularly if you have a permanent participating policy. Then, if you were to become totally disabled tomorrow, you would no longer pay premiums, but your cash value and dividends would continue. How nice. However, I hope you ignore this Mickey Mouse proposition and instead prepare yourself adequately and completely against the shattering possibility that you may become disabled. With adequate disability insurance you would be able to maintain your life insurance.

In addition to the many different types of life insurance you can buy, you can also specify different ways in which the money is to be paid. It can be paid in a lump sum, or in specified amounts over a period of years. The company, of course, would love to keep the money and dole it out. I don't recommend that, but neither is it wise to suddenly dump a large sum of money on a surviving person at this worst of all times. I suggest directing the company to hold the money at interest, subject to withdrawal at any time. This enables the beneficiary to draw what she needs, without pressure.

Chapter 5

How the Industry Grew

Picture five trillion dollars. I don't even care what denomination bills you use. Just imagine $5,000,000,000,000.

Now you know how big the life insurance industry is, because that's the amount of life insurance in force in the United States and Canada today. And it's growing at the rate of more than $700 billion a year.

Life insurance companies have total assets of more than $534 billion. That's more than most countries are worth. The assets of the five largest companies—Prudential is number one, with $60 billion—total more than $185 billion. Seventy-five companies have assets of more than $1 billion.

I could give you a lot more statistics, from *Best's Review,* the Cadillac of trade magazines, from which I got these figures, from the *Life Insurance Fact Book*'s 128 pages of information on every phase of the industry, from *Fortune*'s annual report on the fifty largest life insurance companies in the United States. It's easy to copy down statistics showing how big the insurance industry is.

But I think it's more interesting to show you how it got so big. I know a little old lady, eighty-five years old, who still drives her own automobile, still makes money babysitting. She is also still paying on her insurance policy, $1.86 a week. Somebody talked her into buying that policy when she was seventeen years old. She has been paying on it for sixty-eight years.

Her annual premium for $500 worth of insurance is $96.72. I don't know what savings institutions were paying back then, but let's say she could have gotten 3 percent interest. If she had put just that first year's premium of $96.72 in the savings bank at 3 percent, it would have compounded itself to $500 years ago.

But look what happened to the money the company collected. True, it had to pay out a high percentage of the total premiums to the man who first sold that teen-aged girl an insurance policy she needed like she needed a space suit. It has also paid out a high commission to the agents who have since trudged to her house, winter and summer, to collect that $1.86. Door-to-door collecting is expensive. But I think it's safe to say that after collecting almost $800 in the first eight years, the company would have kept enough to pay the $500 death benefit.

So for the last sixty years this company has had the $500 they promised to pay her for dying. A company smart enough to sell a seventeen-year-old girl a life insurance policy surely has invested that money at more than 3 percent interest. But to be very conservative, let's use that figure—right up to the present, when rates are more than five times as much. And we see that this $500, which is all the company has to pay when she dies, has doubled, then doubled again, and passed $3,000—six times the original amount—in sixty years.

And that represents only the first eight years of premiums.

For although the company had not only collected more than what it promised to pay her sixty years ago, somebody has also kept right on collecting it all over again, year by year, and will continue to collect it until she dies or reaches one hundred. (Or until I step in.) And each year it is invested again at compound interest. By now this amount must be astronomical.

The company has sold her the same product over and over again for sixty-eight years and is still going strong. And the product was only a piece of paper, an IOU, to begin with.

That's why the insurance industry is up to its ears in money.

The little old lady is paying for only one of more than 400 million insurance policies in the United States alone. The number of potential buyers is increasing.

Eighty million Americans were born in the 1945–1965 period; they are coming into the insurance-buying age. A huge new market is being discovered in liberated women. If women can be corporate executives or Supreme Court Justices, they must have some value. Insure them!

And despite an apparent change in lifestyle, there were more marriages than ever before in 1980—2.41 million. People today are still marrying, still securing housing, still having children, still reaching old-fashioned maturity and responsibility. They will continue to buy life insurance.

The industry can't lose. It has billions coming in every year in new premiums, billions coming in from premiums already sold, and billions coming in from the investments of the billions already collected. That's billions times billions times billions.

Out of this enormous income the industry pays back only about $25 billion; $12 billion to beneficiaries and $13 billion to policyholders in dividends, endowments, cash value surrenders, and disability payments.

The industry is foolproof, depression-proof. During the Great Depression the income of the insurance industry was greater than that of the United States. When I first went with Metropolitan, they told us that if the company went bankrupt then the nation had failed the day before.

Insurance companies have so much money that they spend a lot of it on self-glorification. Look at the huge, striking buildings, monuments to insurance companies, in cities all over the country. They spend it on advertising—newspaper, magazine, radio, and especially television. They love to throw money away on television. I think it's an absolute waste. How do I know? Because during all the years I was the manager of offices for three separate companies, I never bothered to provide a chair for a client to sit in. With all that advertising, no prospect ever came in the door.

How many insurance companies are there? I used to think there were 1,800. I was taught that if a prospect ever raised the issue of buying insurance for less, I should reply, "Well, there are 1,800 life insurance companies and, indeed, if you want to try them all, you may die of old age before you get insured."

Browsing through the Bible of the industry recently, *Best's Agent's Guide to Life Insurance Companies,* I saw that there are 1,364 companies ranked by admitted assets, with the last on the list having total assets of $58,000, and 1,293 listed by insurance in force, the last on the list with a total of $2,000. So although *Best's Review* does indeed give the number of life insurance companies as 2,085 at the beginning of 1982, many of these are hardly operational. (About a fourth, 579, were chartered in Arizona.) In 1980, 69 percent of the total of new business was issued by the 100 largest companies. They had 76 percent of the total insurance in force, and 84 percent of the total assets. *Best's Flitcraft Compend,* 1981, lists rates and values for 317 companies, American and Canadian, writing 98 percent of the legal reserve life insurance in force.

Most insurance companies are *stock companies,* owned by people who buy stock in them just as in other corporations. The insurance industry, however, also contains *mutual* companies. There are only about 130 of them, but they have more than half of all the industry assets. And mutual companies are out of this world.

Mutual companies are owned by the policyholders, which means that any illiterate sharecropper paying 25¢ a week for a policy has as much say in the company as the holder of a $1 million policy, or the holder of several policies. They've got one vote. If you have a share of stock in any big corporation, you receive annually a proxy form and an invitation to come to the annual meeting. Some mutual companies invite and encourage you to vote, some don't. In an article in the *Wisconsin Law Review,* the authority on mutual companies, J.A.C. Hetherington, pointed out that of 18,704,879 policyholders of Prudential in 1968, 592 voted in person, one by mail. Of 3,345,479 policyholders of the Equitable Life Insurance Society, 12 showed up in person and 35 voted by mail. And of the more than 22,000,000 policyholders of Metropolitan, none voted at all that year because the company didn't have an election.

If you own a share of stock in a corporation, you can sell it, give it away, or leave it to your children. With your ownership in a mutual insurance company, all you can do is die.

A policy with a mutual company is called *participating,* and it usually costs more than a comparable policy with a stock company. The mutual company doesn't know how many of its owners are going to die in any given year, so it deliberately overcharges in order to be safe. (Can you imagine Prudential, with $60 billion in assets and using the loaded 1958 actuarial table, fretting about not being able to pay off?)

At the end of the year the mutual company management figures out how much of your money it wants to give back. This is your dividend. If you think it is a true dividend, just try to pay taxes on it. The IRS won't take your money. It ruled long ago that a mutual insurance company's dividend is actually a partial refund of an overcharge. Many companies don't give you *anything* back the first year. You're always a year behind.

Some people who have had mutual policies for many years report happily that their dividends have increased steadily. I say, Great! But just imagine how much more they'd be getting every year if they had put an equivalent amount in a decent investment.

Just as mutual policyholders usually don't know they're paying more than non-participating policyholders, few salesmen know what other companies charge. I did happen to know, because I was one of a very few who represented both stock and mutual companies at different stages of my career. But when I was selling mutual policies I sure as hell never told anybody he could buy insurance cheaper at the stock company across the street.

Mutual companies provide printouts for the client showing the amount of the premium and an *estimate* of the dividend. There's no guarantee the company will pay any of that amount. Nevertheless, in selling the policy we deduct the dividend. The resulting figure is what we tell the prospect the policy will cost.

I remember one rare occasion when a prospect told one of my salesmen he could buy insurance cheaper from somebody else. The competitor had a higher premium, but his estimated dividends were higher, too, and resulted in a lower net cost. Well, two could play at that game. The salesman took our company's estimated dividends and *re*-estimated them, right up to where they reduced the net cost of the policy to a very attractive figure. The prospect bought the policy. You want an estimate, you'll get an estimate.

You will probably never know what each year's dividend will be anyway, much less collect it, because the fine print in the application you sign authorizes the company to use the dividends to automatically buy additional high-cost insurance.

Another option pushed by the company is to leave your

dividends on deposit, drawing interest. That's interest of 5 or 6 percent for you; Lord knows what the company is making with your money. I've seen estimates that there are billions of dollars in this type of deposit, making money for the companies, forgotten by the policyholders.

Suppose you were smart enough and stubborn enough to have your dividends deducted from your premium, or even paid to you in cash. In contrast to your nice fat dividend check from your public utilities stock, or your discounted bonds, you're getting a pretty low return. But do not get agitated, because although you are supposed to have just as much say as any other policyholder of the company, including the chairman of the board, there is not one thing you can do about it. A mutual company is not run for its policyholder/owners, it's run for the benefit of the people who run the company. If you own stock in a corporation and you don't like the way it's being managed, you can get a list of the other stockholders, ask them for their proxies, and fire the president. In a mutual insurance company, only the employees can get a list of the policyholders, and the employees can't vote. Hello, square one.

I have a juicy proposal to make to all the readers of this book. Let's all buy a $1,000 policy in any one of the big mutuals, go to the next meeting, and elect me president. I will fire all the sales personnel—there are tens of thousands of them—and close down the sales offices. Then we'll pay ourselves dividends based on the earnings of our investments, undiluted by the expense of selling insurance, which is about 150 percent of the first year's premium.

Whether we're talking about the mutual companies or the stock companies, the insurance industry is clever at marketing its products. It's a shame that it is not working for its policyholders instead of, in so many cases, against them. The industry is ingenious, but this ingenuity is directed toward its own aggrandizement.

In the late nineteenth century, American companies began

looking with envy at the success of the Prudential Assurance Company of London. It had designed small policies for people who could afford a few pence each week, and they sold like fish and chips. An American company named itself The Prudential Insurance Company of America and emulated its big brother across the sea. After several years of success, its stockholders sold it to themselves and made the company mutual. They'd put up less than $100,000 originally; they made $18 million. A $10,000 investment paid $2 million for the stock, $700,000 in dividends.

The Metropolitan Life Insurance Company was even cleverer. It imported several hundred experienced salesmen from England, and turned them loose on working-class prospects. This historical episode reminds me of years later when, as a sales manager under pressure to produce more business, I'd load up my car with salesmen and drive to a low-cost housing development or trailer court. I'd give the boys a little pep talk, and then we'd burst out of the car like Green Berets.

We—all salesmen, all companies—were trained to sell, trained to prey on fear and ignorance, and we sold a lot of insurance that way—always high-cost, permanent insurance. It wouldn't have been worth our trouble to sell anything else. We, and the other companies that operated this way, referred to this operation as "throwing contracts up against the wall and seeing if they'd stick," because more often than not, when the new policyholders came out of hypnosis, they just let their insurance lapse. Even then it was a good deal for the company because it was all one-way money; when the insurance lapsed, the company kept the money and no longer had the obligation to pay the death benefit.

But it was miserable work.

Among the favorite hunting grounds were the communities around the naval base where personnel lived in house trailers. These people really don't have much money, and thanks to military benefits, need less insurance. But they are easy to sell it to. Many soldiers in today's army are practically illiterate. A fast-talking salesman simply overwhelms them. He can imply that the commanding officer will make it tough if they don't buy. And the biggest weapon of all is that military regulations permit the premiums to be deducted from their paycheck. The only other deduction permitted is for savings bonds. Thanks to the insurance lobby, the military opens the door for us to prey on its own people.

The insurance industry stays with the troops like camp followers. I've seen advertisements in trade magazines for agents to sell insurance to military personnel overseas, with commissions as high as 116 percent. It sounded so exciting that when Cathy and I were married, we thought of spending a couple of years in Europe. The company was delighted with the idea and flew us to New York to discuss it. With a New York-based company, my commission would be only 55 percent, but oh, those incentives. My first $20,000 of income would be tax-free. The company would move us, and provide free round-trip transportation back home once a year, plus bonus trips to Spain, Italy, and Greece. We were told that domestic help cost practically nothing. Cathy would live like a princess, bossing her servants around. The idea did have a certain appeal, but we decided to stay home. However, there are lots of other salesmen abroad right now, working for various companies, blackjacking soldiers with third- and fourth-grade educations into buying expensive insurance with the premiums deducted from their paychecks. When you're a trillion-dollar industry, every little bit helps!

Chapter 6

Sell the Sizzle

Every now and then you read an article in the financial press saying that the insurance business is in a shaky position. Don't believe it. The marketing people will always come up with some new tool for smart, aggressive salesmen to sell you insurance.

Because, when you get right down to it, we don't sell you *life insurance*—all that is is money when you're dead. We don't sell a policy; we sell what the policy will do for you.

In our training, in our sales meetings, in our promotional literature, in everything we hear and read about life insurance, it is pounded into us that our mission is saintly. We are the saviors of the widows and orphans of the nation. We protect the American home. Inspiring words?

The most inspiring words I ever heard pertaining to life insurance were *"Sell the sizzle, not the steak."* What a magnificent statement! That sizzle, properly applied, made fortunes for people who sold Sizzlin' Steaks, and it made a good living for me.

If I have to explain *Sell the sizzle, not the steak* to you, I'd advise you not to go into the selling business. What it means is that you don't sell whatever it is you're selling, you sell some gimmick related to it.

I never sold insurance. During my last year as a general agent I represented about forty companies. I carried six business cards and not one had the word "insurance" on it. What I sold was Estate Planning, or Financial Analysis, or Business Continuation Programs. I never even mentioned the word "insurance"—which is one reason why I sold a lot of it.

One of the first sizzles I learned was *the blackout period* in Social Security benefits. I've sold millions of dollars' worth of insurance with *the blackout period*. You are a nice young couple, say, just beginning to realize your responsibilities as citizens, married people, parents. I have made an appointment with you under the pretext of advising you on your personal family finances. I have knocked on the door the way I was taught, introduced myself the way I was taught, opened my briefcase and taken out material the way I was taught, sat you down together on my right the way I was taught. After a brief summary of some of your needs, real and artificial, I lean forward and say, in a voice of gloom and doom:

"And then there is *the blackout period.*"

Whoever thought of that phrase should win the Nobel Prize for Literature. It refers to the period when a widow receives no Social Security payments. It begins when the youngest child reaches sixteen. (Before the 1981 tax law it was eighteen. Salesmen today have two more years to frighten you with. They must be eating high on the hog.) The blackout period—no payments—continues until the mother is sixty years old, when Social Security payments begin again. It is a legitimate concern because it's true that she doesn't collect Social Security during that period. But it's the word *blackout* and my tone of voice that clinch the deal. All the family planning, the careful estimates, the study and decisions that will determine the future of this family— throw them out the window. What people buy is the sizzle, the blackout period.

The blackout period is only one of the standard *needs* memorized in our training sessions—soft points in every person's heart and belly, where we could thrust in a dagger and twist. My company provided a little booklet, *You and Your Family,* with all those needs spelled out. We'd secure an appointment in order to provide, with absolutely no obligation, *Family Security Checkup.* The life insurance agent was presented as being the only person in the whole wide world who looked out for this good American family. Only the agent, compassionate and knowledgeable, could take the time to sit down and calculate just what this fine family might need should that dark day come when they no longer had Dad to provide.

We were trained in identifying needs, in creating needs if they didn't exist—brand-new needs. We were experts in overestimating needs. We painted the future black, then put dollar figures on it.

Final expenses is a good cheerful need to begin with.

How much does it cost to die? We've all heard of lingering deaths. It's bad enough having one, without having to worry about paying for it.

And the funeral. Nobody wants a cheap funeral.

By the time we ticked off hospital expenses, casket, grave, and marker, we'd have a $10,000 need. Do you think I ever gave them a chance to think of their Blue Cross, their major medical, their company benefits? Do you think I ever mentioned my own action in giving my body to a medical school in order to avoid *all* funeral expenses?

Then we'd go on to the *emergency fund.*

"You probably have a savings account, sir," I would say, nodding my head.

He would nod, too. Nobody admits he doesn't have a savings account.

"You certainly want your wife to have an emergency fund should anything happen to you, don't you? She'll need money for the unforeseen emergencies that may come up."

I nod, he nods. It's amazing how you can get anybody to agree with you, just by nodding.

Actually, I've lived forty years without an emergency fund, and my wife can live her life without one too, as far as I'm concerned. Many people feel the same way. But let me tell you, if you're sitting there, looking a man straight in the eye, with his wife by his side, he's not going to say, "Hell, no, I don't care if my wife doesn't have an emergency fund." Chalk up $10,000.

Education for your children.

"Certainly you plan on providing college educations for your three children, sir."

We keep on nodding.

"And you wouldn't want them to be deprived of that opportunity, now would you, if anything should happen to you before that time."

Let the prospect mention that the three-year-old loves to play with his plastic stethoscope, and bingo—there's Harvard Medical School! That will add another $100,000. How many years does it take to be a brain surgeon, anyway?

How about *mortgage insurance?* That's a honey of a sizzle. Let's say there is a $75,000 house with a $40,000 mortgage.

"Certainly you plan on your wife continuing to live in the surroundings and style she's accustomed to?"

Nod. Actually she might be a lot better off leaving the damn thing with its leaky faucets and riding mower that doesn't start. With $35,000 equity in this house already, she could sell it, invest the proceeds, and rent a town house for the rest of her life.

But instead we add $40,000 to the list.

And how about leaving some income for the widow to live on? *Dependency income,* we called it.

All of these needs are for the lucky client who dies. Suppose he lives? Ah, for that eventuality we have *retirement.* That's the noblest need of all, for you get it without dying. It's also the phoniest. Don't buy life insurance to provide retirement income—that's a sizzle! Life insurance is money when you die. Retirement income is money when you're still alive, and life insurance is a poor way to get it. But I've still sold a lot of it just for that purpose, and more millions are being sold every day.

All along I've been rounding figures upward and adding them up. The prospect and I have agreed on each figure; indeed, I encourage him to name each amount himself. When I present the total, therefore, it represents his own way of thinking, however much I may have helped him exaggerate it. Thanks to my list of needs, real and synthetic, we have arrived at a figure. Now all he has to do is take money away from all his other responsibilities and pastimes in order to pay for a permanent, high-cost, probably participating policy for that amount. Of which that hardworking salesman, dedicated to the sizzle—oops, I mean insurance—gets anywhere from 55 to 250 percent.

There are other gimmicks. Marketing schemes come and go in life insurance like hula hoops and discos. I remember the Dominant Needs program. Instead of creating and totaling up several needs, we would present major reasons to have life insurance, one after another, like pulling handkerchiefs out of sleeves. Family Income. Mortgage. Retirement. When we saw the prospect's eyes light up, we'd concentrate on what turned him on, sell it quick, and move on.

Many a time I've parked in front of a prospect's house and decided, at the last minute, purely on impulse, which sizzle to use. Because of that casual whim on my part, the client may have wound up with too much insurance, which was good for me, or too little, which could be a catastrophe for his wife and children.

Just as the insurance industry provides sizzles to sell family insurance at night, so it gives its three-piece-suit agents big-buck, sophisticated sizzles to use where there's more potential. For example, a client to whom I had previously sold a policy opened up a chic, expensive boutique with his wife. He was the business manager; she ran the store. They resisted my offer to increase the amount of his policy and sell her one of her own. So out came a sizzle, the magic phrase, *key-man insurance.*

If anything happened to either of them, I pointed out, the business manager in the office or the store manager up front, the boutique would be in a precarious situation. "It is for this tragic eventuality that we have devised *key-man insurance,*" I said. "Key-man insurance would provide the amount necessary to find and train a new key man, business manager or store manager, and preserve this beautiful boutique you've worked so hard to build."

The commission was 102 percent of $1,735. What sold them was *key man* at $867.50 a word.

On the corporate level, another lovely phrase is *buy/sell agreement.* Under its provisions I sell the corporation a policy on every member for the amount of stock he owns in the corporation—that is, what he would sell the stock for in an arm's length transaction. Now, when one of the owners dies, the corporation collects the insurance and uses that money as per agreement to buy the stock from his widow or other survivors. Otherwise, I point out, she might sell the stock to some outsider, or bring in her brother, the one they dropped on his head when he was a baby, to represent her interests.

Another sizzle is *split-dollar insurance,* a way to reward your key man in lieu of taxable salary. It's expensive insurance.

Nearly all companies have worked out systematic procedures in which you pay more at the beginning in order to borrow on the cash value, with tax-deductible interest, to pay some of the subsequent premiums. This type of arrangement is referred to as *minimum deposit.* It is quite popular, even among otherwise sophisticated individuals.

Retired lives reserve is designed to take care of a large number of people in one organization. The IRS prohibits permanent plans for group insurance, so the insurance industry came up with this gimmick, in which the corporation pays high, permanentlike premiums with the excess over the actual term premium going into a side fund that will continue to pay premiums upon retirement.

There are so many of these gimmicks, and so many different names for them, that one company printed up a glossary. But all of them are only tiny drops of water dancing on the skillet compared to the greatest sizzle of all.

I'm talking about *cash value,* the foundation of the insurance industry.

Let's say that the client, whoever he is, has second thoughts. This is when I pull out Sizzle Numero Uno.

I have had the company print up a ledger statement for me. Here is one, designed for a 25-year-old male with a $100,000 policy.

LEDGER STATEMENT, NON-PAR
FACE VALUE $100,000, ANNUAL PREMIUM $885

End of policy year	Cash value	Cash value increase	Premium less cash value increase	Cumulative premium less cash value	Death benefit
1	$0	$0	$885	$885	$100,000
2	0	0	885	1,770	100,000
3	200	200	685	2,455	100,000
4	1,200	1,000	115CR	2,340	100,000
5	2,200	1,000	115CR	2,225	100,000
10	8,000	1,200	315CR	850	100,000
15	14,600	1,400	515CR	1,325CR	100,000
20	22,400	1,600	715CR	4,700CR	100,000
40	56,600	1,600	715CR	21,200CR	100,000

We sit down comfortably, each with a copy of the ledger statement.

"I want you to look at these figures carefully, sir," I say. "The first column shows you how long you've had the policy. The second shows the guaranteed cash value. This is money you can always get simply by asking for it. Next you see how much your cash value increases each year.

"Now let me call your attention to line four, the fourth year. At this point you already have a cash value of $1,200. Look at the cash value increase—one thousand dollars. That's more than the premium! You're getting this policy free! See, the next column shows you're actually getting a credit of a hundred and fifteen dollars. Go on down that column of figures. See it increase. It's like taking money out of your left-hand pocket and putting it in your right—with interest."

By now he's hooked. But I don't let up.

"Here's another way of looking at it. See year fifteen? $14,600. Let me work this out on my calculator—$885 times times fifteen is $13,275. That's how much you've put in, and already the cash value is more. Now you're making money. Look at line twenty. You've got a cash value of $22,400. That's $4,700 more than you put in."

I've sold a lot of insurance this way. I've never had anyone question these figures. Indeed, the figures are completely accurate—as far as they go.

But look at some of the fallacies.

- If his cash value increases so much more than his premium each year, why does he have to keep shelling out money?
- In the first three years he put up $885 three times, but only $200 was credited to his cash value.
- What *is* cash value, anyway? If you die—which is why you bought the insurance, isn't it?—you get the face value, not the cash value. If you borrow the cash value, you pay interest. If you take it all, which means cashing in your policy, you forfeit the rest of your life insurance.

- You do not see my commission here. On the first $885 premium, my commission was $902.70. That's right, $902.70. One hundred two percent. After that, I got 15 percent the second year, then ten. It decreases, but as long as you keep paying, I keep collecting.
- But the biggest bit of hocus-pocus is this: These figures brush right over the time value of money. When you turn over your $885 to the company each year, you lose the use of it. The company gains the use of it.

In the business this is known as the *net cost method*.

"Look at this, sir!" I say, as though I had just discovered it myself. "Look at year forty, age sixty-five. After forty years you will have a cash value of $56,600. Follow that across— $21,200 *more* than the total of your premiums, more than you put in! And you've still got your $100,000 policy to protect your loved ones, just in case."

People smart enough to hold good jobs, make good money, fall for that line. They still do because, don't let anybody fool you, the net cost method of selling life insurance is still Number One. To make it simple, if you give me $1,000 a year for ten years you have given me more than $10,000. You have also given me the use of it, and I have therefore invested it at compound interest.

Even at a piddling 5 percent I've turned your $1,000 a year into more than $13,000 after ten years.

So, getting back to the ledger statement, we see that these figures are not applicable. The premium of $885 paid for forty years does not total $35,400 in the real world. Invested at 5 percent a year, it becomes more than $110,000. *That* is the true amount you put up to get your cash value of $56,600 —which the company will lend you at 6 percent interest.

It would be hard to beat the cash value sizzle, but the insurance industry did make a good try with estate-tax insurance. Who else could have figured a way to step in between the taxpayer and the United States Treasury and intercept the flow of billions?

This sizzle goes by many names—financial analysis, estate planning, estate liquidity; but whatever you call it, it's based on cash value insurance. Prospects are easy to find.

Many a beautiful sunny morning I've taken a ride in the country and located a farm that in the past few years has quadrupled in value. Or I could just walk into some prosperous, privately owned business. Inflation has created many unsuspecting millionaires. But another surprise, less pleasant, will be the amount of tax the heirs will have to pay to inherit the inflated estate. Actually, the government will permit the heirs to pay the estate taxes over a period of fifteen years, with no tax payments at all, just 4 percent interest on the principal, over the first five years. But nobody knows that.

As a Chartered Life Underwriter and estate planner I could establish Centers of Influence simply by taking every important attorney, certified public accountant, and trust officer to lunch. Lawyers and CPAs were more than willing for me to bring in clients at $50 an hour. Trust officers were happy to receive new accounts.

If they were aware that I was selling expensive insurance on commission, they did not volunteer that information to the client. *Nobody,* not even the lawyer who sends you a bill, protects you from the insurance salesman.

I explained to every client that by paying a few cents on the dollar now, in the form of life insurance premiums, he would save a great deal more later. Not one realized that no matter how much he did or did not put up now, it would not cost him one plugged nickel later. He could be worth zillions and he still wouldn't pay a cent in inheritance tax.

How could he? He'd be dead.

Nobody I ever worked with caught that difference. Nobody ever realized it was not a matter of *him* spending now versus *him* spending more later. Rather, it was *him* spending now and *somebody else* spending later. This guy is leaving his wife, his children, whoever, a few million bucks—let them pay the taxes. They're getting the money.

Estate-tax insurance was certainly one of the cleverest inventions of the life insurance industry. Fortunes were made in it. The government would get its money in the end, but in the meantime the insurance company would have the use of it, the salesman would get a large commission, the heirs would get the estate intact, and the poor sucker who paid the inflated premiums never realized he'd been taken. How wonderful for everybody.

With every wealthy person a potential golden goose, it's amazing to me that the industry let this provision be so drastically gutted in the Tax Act of 1981, effective 1982. It must have whipped through Congress before the powerful insurance lobby realized what was happening. The act wiped out the inheritance taxes on many estates immediately. Under its provisions anyone who is married can simply leave everything to the spouse, tax-free. For the unmarried, and those who wish to leave large amounts to other inheritors, taxes will decrease steadily until 1987, when all estates up to $600,000 will be tax-free.

Or will they? Surely by that time the insurance industry will either have inheritance taxes back in the books, doubled in spades, or some other gimmick to enable its salesmen to start bringing in the billions again.

In the meantime, if you are in the enviable position of having an estate on which someone is going to have to pay taxes, refer to Chapter 15 for how much insurance you need.

If you need any at all. This is one tax you're not going to be around to pay.

Chapter 7

The FTC Bites the Dust

If you think it extreme to predict that the insurance industry will lobby some kind of deal through Congress to make up for its lost tax insurance, you just haven't been keeping up with the running battle between the industry and the government. So far the industry has a big lead.

A skirmish of particular interest happened a century ago in Massachusetts. A fellow named William S. Manning published the complete record of the 1877 investigation of the insurance industry. The companies bought up the entire printing and gave Manning an annual retainer for the rest of his life. If you're reading this, it didn't happen to Random House and me.

The federal government got into the insurance action after antitrust legislation was passed. In 1944 the Supreme Court said what ought to be obvious to anybody: insurance transactions were interstate commerce, and therefore subject to federal antitrust laws. The industry put an end to that nonsense.

Within a year it had lobbied the McCarran-Ferguson Act through Congress, providing that federal laws apply to insurance only if it is not regulated by state law. To put it bluntly, Congress told itself and other federal agencies to lay off the insurance industry. That's why I said earlier in this book that there is more federal control over a jelly bean than there is over any insurance policy you've got.

Who does regulate insurance? Insurance commissioners in the fifty states, the District of Columbia, Puerto Rico, the Virgin Islands, and Guam. People in the insurance industry say, "Well, it's better to be regulated by fifty-four monkeys than by King Kong." Regulations vary from state to state, with the National Association of Insurance Commissioners (NAIC) making some effort to standardize them. There's another saying in the industry that commissions are staffed by insurance company trainees or retirees.

With experience as a life insurance salesman and manager in three different states, I was aware that there were commissioners, but they didn't bother me one way or the other. Neither I, my salesmen, nor my clients had any idea of what state regulation, rather than federal regulation, meant to any of us. One result, I know now, is that because of the cozy relationship and the lack of competition between insurance companies, the life insurance purchaser can pay fantastically different premiums for the same amount of insurance. It's still hard for me to realize today that as a licensed broker with rate cards from about forty companies in my file, I can sell $100,000 worth of insurance for $100 or $4,000, depending upon which application I pull out of my drawer.

Let me give you an analogy. You are standing with your real estate agent in a nice subdivision looking at one side of a duplex for sale. It costs $250,000. The other side of the duplex, identical in every way, is for sale, too, but by another agent. Only after you have bought your side of the house, moved in, and met the guy who just bought the other side, do you discover that while you paid $250,000, he paid $50,000. Can you picture such a scenario? Can you imagine such a discrepancy in prices for identical houses, without you or your agent knowing it? Well, in insurance it happens every minute.

If you find it hard to believe this, you're not alone. An economist named Michael P. Lynch told me that even after writing his dissertation on an insurance topic for his Ph.D. at the University of Chicago he was under the impression that people who buy life insurance investigate the market and select the policy that is best suited for them. Not until he was actually teaching at the University of Indiana, under the consumerist authority Joseph M. Belth, did he discover, through studying actual rate books, that premiums varied widely, that clients bought what they were sold. People began coming to him for advice, and by the time he had moved on to the Federal Trade Commission in Washington, he figured he had saved people thousands of dollars in insurance premiums. He found himself in an ironic situation: although he was an advocate of low-cost group insurance, he advised people under the age of fifty *not* to buy Federal Employee Group Life Insurance because he considered it rigged to provide benefits for older employees and retirees (and the companies that write it) at the expense of the younger.

Inasmuch as the FTC has many consumer protection programs, like Truth in Lending, and making cigarette companies tell you how much tar and nicotine you're inhaling, Lynch began pushing for activity in the area of life insurance. He wound up with a task force of about eight people and a work load of seventy or seventy-five hours a week.

The results were released in July 1979 in the form of a staff report entitled "Life Insurance Cost Disclosure." It's an inch and a quarter thick and weighs three pounds. It began with the statement that "no other product in our economy that is purchased by so many people for so much money is bought with so little understanding of its actual or comparative value."

So how did the FTC set about making it understandable? First it examined a method worked out some years before by the National Association of Insurance Commissioners by which one policy could be compared with another. The method was included in the NAIC Model Bill presented to state legislatures; thirty-four had adopted it by 1981.

In an obvious effort to forestall consumer criticism, the NAIC made it possible to assign to every life insurance policy an index number representing a simple means of comparison. It would be included in a Buyer's Guide, issued with the policy.

You remember that I told you about *net cost.* I would show the client a ledger statement comparing the cash value of the policy at a given year with the total amount he had paid in premiums. As the net cost method ignores completely the time value of money, it does not provide an accurate means of comparison. So the NAIC proposed the *interest-adjusted method* of comparing policies. It chose two time spans, ten and twenty years. Here's how this method works.

Take the accumulated amount of premiums, compounded at 5 percent, at the end of ten years. Subtract the cash value from that figure. This is the *interest-adjusted net cost.* To arrive at an index, divide that number by 13.207 ($1 a year invested at 5 percent equals $13.207). Now you have the *interest-adjusted net cost index* for a ten-year period. To get the index for twenty years, repeat the process, dividing by 34.717. These index numbers represent the annual investment required to build up a sum equal to the interest-adjusted net cost in two periods of time, ten and twenty years. Every cash value policy has its index numbers for you to compare. The lower the numbers, the better the policy.

Those indices, for ten and twenty years, are based on cash value. Suppose that instead of taking your cash value, you die. That's what insurance is for, isn't it? Okay, we work that out, too, for ten and twenty years, in the same manner except that we do not subtract cash value. Cash value disappears when you die. We call these figures the interest-adjusted net *payment* indices.

If the policies are participating, which pay dividends, the accumulated dividends (estimated and compounded at 5 percent, of course) must first be subtracted from the accumulated premiums.

Many companies had their actuaries deliberately jiggle their ten- and twenty-year figures so that the indices looked good at the expense of other years.

To crown this exercise in chicanery, the Buyer's Guide, which contains these figures, is not shown to the client until *after* he agrees to buy the insurance. It is delivered with the policy. Studies have shown that about 1 percent of insurance buyers look at the indices at that point. If a buyer does look at them and understand them, and decides he wants to cancel the whole thing, he's got a ten-day cooling off period in which he can get his money back. There's a sticker attached to the policy telling him so.

The sticker is very easy to remove.

You can see why an NAIC committee recommended in 1981 that the interest-adjusted method be dropped.

To return to the FTC task force, it reached the conclusion early in its study that the interest-adjusted method did not provide a means of comparing one insurance policy with another. Insurance purchasers didn't know that some policies cost more than others. Indeed, as I've said before, *agents* didn't know; a 1976 survey showed that 37 percent of full-time agents and 45 percent of supervisors believed that "there's little difference in net cost for similar policies."

In order to compare policies on an accurate basis, therefore, the FTC chose a different method, the Linton Yield. This is a way to separate that part of an insurance premium that applies to the insurance protection from that part that applies to savings—the cash value. With dividends also involved, the equations necessary would drive Einstein up a wall. The task force obtained policies from about 150 companies and fed the material into an IBM 370 computer.

Working with the Linton Yield, the task force arrived at several conclusions. Here are some of them:

Of the premium dollar, only 15 cents goes to death benefits. Overhead gets 30 cents, and the remaining 55 cents, over half of every dollar paid in premiums, goes into the savings component.

The average return paid to the consumer on the savings component, or cash value, was about 1.3 percent. That's a shockingly low figure, but it includes both the zero cash value accrued by most policies in the first year or two, and the low cash value accrued in the next few years.

Even in insurance policies held for many years, interest rates were low and diverse. Participating $25,000 policies issued to males aged thirty-five showed a twenty-year rate of return ranging from 1.5 percent to 7.6 percent, and for nondividend paying policies, the scale ranged from 0.66 percent to 3.9 percent. The report did not name specific companies. Later, however, the *Hartford Courant,* through a Freedom of Information Act request, obtained the FTC staff figures for several insurance companies including the two largest in the United States. The *Courant* printed them on February 10, 1980, as follows:

- Connecticut General: 3.2 percent after 20 years, minus 0.2 percent after 10 years, and minus 12.9 percent after five years.
- Connecticut Mutual: 5.1 percent after 20 years, 3.7 percent after 10 years, and minus 7.5 after five years.
- Phoenix Mutual: 6.7 percent after 20 years, 5.9 percent after 10 years, and zero after five years.
- Travelers Corp.: 3.3 percent after 20 years, 0.2 percent after 10 years, and minus 14 percent after five years.

- Prudential Insurance Co. of America: 3.9 percent after 20 years, 0.9 percent after 10 years, and minus 6.5 percent after five years.
- Metropolitan Life Insurance Co.: 3.3 percent after 20 years, minus 0.6 percent after 10 years, and minus 13.8 percent after five years.

The *Courant* pointed out that passbook savings were paying 5.25 percent interest, and tax-free municipal bonds were paying 5.2 percent.

The FTC report pointed out that price competition is so ineffective in insurance that the lowest paying companies competed successfully with the highest.

It also included a large section on pension plans. I'll summarize it, as follows: If you're thinking of setting up your pension plan through an insurance company, don't.

During the time the FTC was working on the report, the insurance industry paid little attention. Such things had been started before and went nowhere, and the industry was fully protected by the McCarran Act anyway. But when the report was introduced with great fanfare at a Senate committee hearing, it made waves. The FTC's criticisms of the industry were convincing. Its major recommendation, a system of cost disclosure to encourage price competition in life insurance, was most reasonable. The report got another boost when President Jimmy Carter sent a letter to all state governors asking for their cooperation in promoting cost disclosure and price competition. The *New York Times* published a strong editorial endorsing cost disclosure.

But what all this added up to was, it made the industry mad. The lobbyists set out to undo the FTC's mischief and do in the FTC. And they knew how to do it. Another Senate hearing was held, and this time the industry was in control. It produced some of its prominent leaders to shoot down the FTC and its report.

And guess who headed up the Senate subcommittee on

consumerism. Wendell H. Ford, former governor of Kentucky, former Jaycee national president, and former very successful insurance salesman.

Senator Ford proposed a bill stomping the hell out of the FTC. The final act, approved by both houses and signed by the President, was a brutal congressional put-down of an executive bureau and an all-out victory for the industry. The actual wording doesn't sound as harsh as it really is. It authorizes the FTC "to conduct studies and prepare reports relating to the business of insurance" *only* "upon receiving a request which is agreed to by a majority of the members" of the House or Senate Commerce Committees.

But it will be one cold day in July when that happens.

And so the insurance industry, already protected from regulation by Act of Congress, now became protected from investigation by Act of Congress. Surely no other industry even approaches such ruthless power.

That was back in 1979. Three years later, Mike Lynch, who worked on it with such dedication, said the report did have some positive results. "Some of the same companies which sent their top men to Washington to claim that insurance is not savings," he observed, "are now taking full-page ads to announce the new interest rates they're paying. That's a 180-degree switch. The report must have had *something* to do with it."

How can I, a conservative Republican opposed in general to governmental control of free enterprise, write so approvingly of the FTC report? After all, when it came out I was an active and successful general agent. What little I knew of the report came from bitter criticism in industry publications, which I accepted completely. Its endorsement by President Jimmy Carter, a liberal Democrat, made it all the more objectionable.

Well, after thinking it over, I don't believe my position on some degree of federal regulation of insurance is inconsistent. I have accepted all along, with a feeling of security, federal

controls over the banks I kept my money in, over the marketing of stocks and bonds I bought. Compared to the enormous, almost secret amount of commission the life insurance
salesman gets, the federally controlled percentages of securities salesmen are almost pathetic—but stockbrokers manage
to do all right. They certainly have a high degree of public
trust and respect, which is more than I can say for the life
insurance sales force as a whole.

As for life insurance itself, I believe that there should be
some federal control over the millions of policies sold each
year. The government swings into action against fruit flies in
oranges and botulism in cans, as well as defects in little cars
and big planes. Why should there not be some reasonable
specifications set for life insurance?

So powerful is the grip of the insurance industry on Congress, however, that it will be some time before any regulation is forthcoming. We have plenty of time to determine just
what those regulations should be.

In the meantime, it's ironic to note that a few complaints
about state regulation are beginning to come from, of all
people, spokesmen for the industry itself. The July 1981 issue
of *Best's Review* quoted Robert M. Best, chairman of a mutual company: "State regulation of the life industry is becoming more of a burden than a benefit for both the life company
and the policyholder. Almost everyone going to a state insurance department will find it difficult to get any understanding
of the real world . . . we all end up with a hodge-podge of
regulation and a very expensive way of doing business. I
think perhaps the time has come for federal regulation to
replace state regulation."

But don't hold your breath.

Chapter 8

They Shouldn't Have Done It to Donahue

The Phil Donahue show is my favorite TV talk show. I think Donahue is just great. His topics are nearly always enlightening and he stays on top of the subject, asks intelligent questions, and gets through the verbiage to the heart of the matter.

But he should never have taken on the insurance industry.

On August 16, 1979, Donahue's guests were two consumer-oriented critics of permanent insurance. The insurance industry was infuriated. They asked for equal time to make *their* case and they got it.

So on September 28 the guests on the Donahue show were Thomas J. Wolff, president of the National Association of Life Underwriters (NALU) and an agent in Connecticut, and Robert A. Beck, chairman and chief executive officer of Prudential. I have seen these fellows operate before, at conventions and gatherings, and I can tell you they are heavyweights. They are tremendous speakers, smooth, clever, convincing. They speak without notes, handle questions on their feet. I'd hate to go up against them.

But I had confidence in Donahue. I settled back to enjoy the show.

Donahue gave them a good introduction. Mr. Beck— that's the way I think of him, *Mister* Beck—was first. He looked and talked like the head of a billion-dollar outfit. You knew he knew his business. He articulated the industry position easily and sincerely, saying that young people should indeed have a great deal of their insurance in term, but that permanent was what they needed later in life.

Insurance really isn't an investment, he said. And then he went right on to say that he had had a policy for twenty-six years and it has provided a rate of return of 4.4 percent. He contradicted himself already! I waited for Donahue to pounce.

But instead Donahue got back to term insurance. "The facts of life," he said, "are that when the enthusiastic, aggressive, courteous life insurance agent calls on newlyweds, he isn't selling term, he's selling whole life."

"Your facts are wrong," Beck said bluntly. I perked up my ears at that. If there is one thing I know about insurance, it is that the insurance salesman, for Prudential as much as for anybody else, is trained to sell whole life. But Beck just sat there and said, "Your facts are wrong." He exuded such confidence, such authority, I almost believed him myself. Donahue sure did.

Beck said very few young people buy term insurance alone. "Most of them buy a permanent policy with a term rider."

Well, I know why. His salesmen, just like any other company's salesmen, sell all the high-priced permanent they can, then tack on the term. Mr. Beck made it sound like this was a beneficent practice with nothing but the young folks' best interests in mind.

Now Tom Wolff broke in. (I think of him as Tom Wolff,

your friendly life insurance agent.) He is intense, dynamic. You can just tell he's a great salesman. Wolff explained that first the salesman establishes how much insurance a person needs, then how much he can afford to pay. He set up an imaginary 35-year-old client who needs $100,000 life insurance, but who can only afford to pay $250. Wolff said that he would recommend term insurance. So far so good. But then he went on.

"Let's take the case of the person who is going to spend $250," Wolff said. "The commission that companies pay varies. Some companies pay a slightly higher commission on ordinary whole life than on term. In my own company, I would make $100 commission in the first year on that term policy I sold for $250. That $100 commission is for the first year only. Let's assume that instead of buying $100,000 term with $250, that person bought $20,000 of whole life for the same price. My commission on whole life would be $125. So I would be $25 better off selling whole life.

"I have been in this business a long time." (He is so sincere, so believable. You know that you can trust this good man with everything you've got.) "Last year, 80 percent of the life insurance I sold was to existing clients. Almost the entire balance was to people who were referred by those clients. In our business, just like any business, we have to build a clientele. You build that clientele by doing what is best for them, not by making an extra $25 commission."

I almost applauded. Although I thought that what he was doing was reprehensible, it was nevertheless what I had been doing for seventeen years, and he was doing it so well. But surely he wouldn't fool Donahue.

I was wrong. Donahue swallowed it hook, line, and sinker.

So did the studio audience. Not one person raised a question.

And I bet that very few of the viewers of the show, telecast on more than 150 stations over the country, realized that Wolff was making fools out of them—and Donahue.

How about you? Look back over what he said. Do you see how, like a sleight-of-hand artist, he distracted your attention with one figure and fooled you with another? If you don't see the trick, be prepared to pay through the nose for your insurance.

Here is what he did. First he set up the client's needs—$100,000 worth of insurance, premium $250 for term insurance, commission $100. Then he said that for the same amount of premium, $250, the client can get $20,000 worth of whole life, and the commission on that is only $125, so it's only a difference of $25 . . .

Wait a minute! What happened to the $100,000 insurance the man needs? Suddenly he was talking about $20,000 instead. He had us comparing apples with oranges—and nobody caught it!

You got taken, Donahue. So did your audience and viewers. And so, for that matter, did all the beneficiaries of all the thousands, perhaps millions, of survivors of insured persons who have been sold smaller amounts of permanent insurance so that salesmen like Wolff and me could make a higher commission. I've played that trick hundreds of times as a salesman, okayed it thousands of times as a manager.

Let's look at it again in detail.

The man needs $100,000 worth of insurance. He can only afford $250. That will buy $100,000 worth of term insurance. But the salesman only gets $100 commission.

For permanent insurance we get a higher commission. Wolff said he would get $125 for the $250 premium on a whole life policy—that's 50 percent. I can't believe that's all a salesman as successful as Tom Wolff gets. Surely the president of the NALU would do better than fifty.

Whatever his commission rate, what Wolff did was to give us the same premium for permanent and term, $250, and use that figure to show he only made $25 more commission to sell whole life. So he has little incentive to push it.

But he is comparing the commission on $100,000 worth of

term insurance to the commission on $20,000 worth of permanent insurance. He said the client needs $100,000. To make a true comparison, he's got to compare the premium for $100,000 worth of term insurance to the premium for *$100,000 worth of permanent insurance,* not $20,000 worth of permanent insurance.

The premium for $100,000 of permanent insurance is going to run $1,300 or more, the commission $750 or more.

Don't tell me Tom Wolff doesn't have incentive to sell a whole life policy!

And don't tell me he did what was best for his clients, either. Here's a client who, Tom Wolff admits on TV in front of millions of people, needs $100,000 worth of life insurance.

What does Tom Wolff sell him? $20,000 worth. Here he is, insurance salesman, president of the NALU, representing the industry on the Donahue show, and he admits he deprives his client of $80,000 worth of death benefits. What happens when that client dies, and his widow tries to take care of herself and her children on the income from $20,000 instead of $100,000?

And how many real life people are trying to get by on a small amount of expensive insurance their husbands left them, when for the same amount of money in term insurance premiums they could have been adequately insured?

After Wolff's magic trick, Beck stepped in again with a flat statement to the effect that in his company the agent's commission for a $250 premium, whether for a term policy or whole life, is almost exactly the same. "I want to state as strongly and unequivocally as I can that the financial motivation for the agent to sell term insurance as compared with whole life does not exist."

What a farce! Ridiculous! I don't care how strongly and unequivocally he states it, it just ain't so.

The Prudential commissions for term and whole life are *not* the same. Prudential agents I know get 55 percent on some whole life policies, 50 percent on others. They get 50 percent on a decreasing term policy, but only 25 percent on annual renewable term.

And even if the percentages *were* the same, it doesn't mean anything. I called a friend at Prudential and learned that for $100,000 face value, the premium for term insurance is about $400, whole life $1,750. Which would you rather have 50 percent of? And Mr. Beck says the financial motivation for selling perm does not exist. In a pig's eye it does not exist.

None of this was surprising. The insurance industry has been confusing the public for centuries. And Beck and Wolff are masters of their art.

But I wish they hadn't done it to Donahue.

Chapter 9

The Kenton Method

The NAIC used the interest-adjusted net cost/payment index, the FTC staff used the Linton Yield, and Consumers Union, assisted by Mike Lynch, master of the Linton Yield, used both.

I've subscribed to *Consumer Reports* for years. I would never dream of buying a stereo component it didn't recommend, nor would Cathy purchase an appliance without consulting it.

But for life insurance, forget it. CU's lengthy articles in the February and March 1980 issues, and the Fourth Edition of its book, the *Consumers Union Report on Life Insurance,* tell you in CU's solemn prose more than you want to know about every phase of life insurance and then list the comparative prices of 478 policies from 110 companies. There are separate lists for permanent and term insurance, from lowest cost to highest, in alphabetical order with symbols showing CU's ratings.

You'd think 110 companies would be enough to choose from, but CU's list is too restrictive. Insurance companies are rated by the A. M. Best Company on a basis of several criteria including adequate reserves and net resources. Those meeting Best's standards are classified A+, A, B+, B, C+, and C. As far as you and I are concerned, however, I think they're all equally good in that they will pay off when we die. What else matters?

CU, however, lists only companies with a rating of A+ and A. I know of several companies that offer less expensive term policies than those listed by CU. Thus, CU's policies could hardly be best buys.

And I object to the CU text for the simple reason that I had to wade through every word of it. It's too much.

These painstaking ratings of permanent insurance are totally unnecessary—unless you're a masochist with a most expensive policy. Listing best buys in permanent insurance is a contradiction in terms. All permanent insurance is a worst buy. Later on I will show why.

My objections to the ratings of term insurance are more complex. Incidentally, CU does recommend term insurance over permanent insurance, but not as forcefully as it should. It also advises you to listen to "an informed and thoughtful agent." Why? If he's thoughtful and informed he's going to sell you the insurance that pays him for being thoughtful and informed. And that isn't term.

CU's criteria for rating term policies are the cost indices for periods of twenty, nine, nineteen, and twenty-nine years, in that order. At first glance that seems to be a good idea; it exposes the companies that suck you in with low rates now only to slap you with high ones later.

But let's examine this further. I'll show you how to have the insurance and the face value in much less than twenty years.

You don't buy insurance for a planned, scheduled demise in a certain number of years, but for an untimely death, a

death that suddenly and unexpectedly deprives your dependents of your support. Buy as much term insurance as they
will need, at the lowest price you can get it for. Suppose in
the next few years the premium jumps in comparison to
another term policy? Do what you would do with any other
commodity. Unload it and get the better buy.

Or suppose, as is almost certain to happen as insurance
companies become more competitive, some other company
reduces its rates? Again, get the better buy. Don't lock yourself into a twenty-year insurance program. Stay flexible. Take
advantage of the insurance industry rather than let it take
advantage of you. Have the lowest cost insurance on your
block.

Some may object to the idea of buying anything described as inexpensive, low-priced, competitive. With insurance, cheap doesn't mean inferior. I like Aramis soap at six
bucks a cake, and I listen to Willie Nelson on Acoustic
Research AR-9 speakers—the cartridge on my turntable
cost $180. I like quality things and I'm willing to pay for
them.

But $100,000 of life insurance is $100,000 worth of life
insurance, no matter what you pay for it. I prefer to pay as
little as possible.

Another reaction I often hear to my method is: *What if my
health deteriorates and I become uninsurable? Then I won't
be able to get a new insurance policy.* My answer is, Always
buy *renewable* term insurance, which the company guarantees to renew at scheduled rates for a specified number of
years. Second, to the complaint that in that case you may be
stuck with a policy that becomes more expensive, all I can
say is, my friend, if you are uninsurable, you probably won't
live long enough for it to make any difference.

As opposed to the NAIC method, the CU method, or any
other system of buying insurance, I therefore propose the
Walter S. Kenton method: Buy the least expensive renewable

term policy available, year after year, until you no longer need it. My method is so simple that I know I will have to defend it at length, as well as show you implicitly how to implement it.

So read on, and I will help you provide for your dependents at less cost to yourself.

Chapter 10

How Much Money Do You Want to Pay?

Most people are under the impression that you buy insurance the same way you buy a car or a house or a box of breakfast cereal. You think you pay for what you get.

That isn't true at all. You pay for what the insurance company and the salesman get.

When you're buying cars you can look at a $25,000 Mercedes and a $5,000 Chevy and tell the difference. When you're buying insurance, you can pay wildly different amounts of money in premiums for the same face value—the same amount of money when you die.

A 25-year-old woman who doesn't smoke cigarettes can buy $100,000 worth of insurance for as little as $106. The same amount of insurance in a *guaranteed issue* policy—the company guarantees to sell it to you, no matter what your physical condition is—would cost a person the same age $18,675.

That's 176 times as much for the same thing, and you still have to die to collect!

Many companies have different rate structures within their own assortment of plans. Insurance salesmen do well to know their own company's range of products and probably neither know nor care what the other companies offer. In any event, no matter whom he represents, the salesman is going to try to sell you expensive cash value insurance.

I know how little other salesmen know about what's available throughout the industry because I remember well my own experience. When I left Metropolitan in 1978, I took with me a $100,000 annual renewable convertible term policy, on which my annual premium at the age of 35 was $334. I thought that was a good policy. How could I think otherwise? That's what the company offered. I never even thought of pricing term insurance.

After I set up as a general agent, I looked into the term policy offered by my principal company, and found it to be no improvement.

Then one day a broker from another town came by, and I just happened to glance at one of the rate cards he left. It was from a company called Standard Security Life Insurance Company of New York. It offered an annual renewable convertible and revertible policy at my age for $183.

This was the lowest priced insurance I had ever seen. As a matter of fact, after fifteen years in the business, I had no idea that a premium could be anywhere near that low. Yet the company was perfectly respectable, with an A rating from Best's and a billion and a half worth of insurance in force.

Since that time I have run across other companies with comparable rates, but only because I have gone out of my way to look for them. If I had remained in the business I would not have searched for lower cost policies, nor would it have been worth my time to sell one—25 percent commis-

As of 1981 every single one of the figures below purchased the same thing: $100,000 if you die. Find the age closest to your own and follow it across. Which amount do you want to pay?

Some figures are projections of smaller amounts of life insurance, some are projections of monthly premium payments. Some include waiver of premium. Thus there may be a discrepancy of a few dollars. All rates are subject to change.

Age	1(T)	2(T)	3(T)	4(T)	5(T)	6(P)!	7(T)	8(T)	9(T)	10(T)	11(T)
25	83	106	112	126	136	139	158	186	202	204	211
30	97	112	112	146	153	141	158	197	224	216	232
35	133	112	117	178	194	143	168	219	282	276	297
40	208	117	142	267	287	183	264	293	420	420	438
45	337	142	175	434	437	237	385	414	649	648	677
50	525	175	251	664	701	321	571	637	1,001	996	1,054
55	812	251	350	1,127	1,170	475	987	1,003	1,490	1,632	1,641
60	1,017	350	531	1,920	1,487	721	1,626	1,667	2,491	2,448	N/A
65	1,017	531	869	N/A	N/A	1,264	N/A	3,331	3,768	4,020	N/A

1. Group insurance for American Statistical Association. Annual renewable term (ART). Fifty percent first-year dividend deducted.

2. Standard Security Life Insurance Company of New York. Female nonsmoker. Annual renewable, revertible and convertible term, non-participating.

3. Standard Security Life Insurance Company of New York. Male nonsmoker. Annual renewable, revertible and convertible term, non-participating.

4. Manhattan Life Insurance Company, ART, nonsmokers' discount, $100 first year discount. Your second year premium would not only go up, but would go up another $100.

5. Teachers' Insurance and Annuity Association, five-year renewable term (5YT), dividend deducted. Rated least costly by Consumers Union, participating.

6. First Colony Life Insurance Company. This, believe it or not, is permanent insurance. The premium goes sky-high later on, but for the first few years it's hard to beat.

7. Massachusetts Savings Bank Life Insurance, nonsmokers' ART, projected from maximum available, $50,000.

8. North American Company for Life and Health Insurance, ART. Rated least costly by Consumers Union, non-participating.

9. Group insurance for Shell Oil Company credit card holders, ART. Note differences with other term policies in advanced years.

You can estimate the cost per thousand by moving the decimal two spaces to the left. ($100 = $1.00 per thousand.) Whenever anyone tries to sell you insurance, compare the cost per thousand with the appropriate figures on this chart.

Or compare this to what you are already paying.

(T) stands for term insurance, (P) stands for permanent.

12(T)	13(T)	14(T)	15(T)	16(P)	17(P)	18(P)	19(P)	20(P)	Age
240	258	509	648	925	1,769	2,485	4,176	18,675	25
266	282	605	653	1,115	2,019	2,795	4,219	22,611	30
322	354	811	648	1,367	2,338	3,146	4,309	27,013	35
432	522	1,123	953	1,700	2,753	3,567	4,455	32,016	40
557	786	1,615	1,330	2,128	3,290	4,061	4,670	35,351	45
780	1,218	N/A	1,818	2,712	3,939	4,684	4,982	38,686	50
1,198	1,962	N/A	2,873	3,493	4,714	5,542	5,474	45,356	55
1,863	3,030	N/A	3,185	4,533	5,864	6,755	6,221	55,361	60
N/A	3,306	N/A	5,803	5,961	7,430	8,511	7,382	70,035	65

10. Group insurance for American Express card holders, ART, projected from maximum available, $50,000.

11. Visa card holders, ART.

12. New York Savings Bank life insurance. Five-year renewable term. Projected from $30,000 maximum available. Price reflects five-year average dividend return.

13. Group insurance, 5YT, for Alumni Associations of several universities, written through National Insurance Administrators for Northwestern National Life Insurance Company.

14. Gerber Life Insurance Company. This is a *term* policy. Projected from maximum of $20,000. Wow.

15. Deposit ART, Fireman's Fund American Life Insurance Company.

16. Massachusetts Savings Bank Life Insurance, straight life, participating, projected from maximum available, $53,000.

17. Fidelity Life Association of Illinois. Whole life policy rated most costly by Consumers Union.

18. Metropolitan Life Insurance Company, twenty-payment life, participating.

19. Fidelity Bankers' Life Insurance Company, twenty-year endowment.

20. Presidential Life Insurance Company. Guaranteed issue. Projected. See text.

sion on $183 is $45.75. However, it was a good deal for me, and I took out $100,000 worth on me, $50,000 for Cathy.

Next year, 1981, would have been an even better deal, for the company decreased rates across the board. The reduced figures are shown in the comparison table.

The most expensive insurance I know of is No. 20 on the table, *guaranteed issue*, which I mentioned earlier. A $100,000 face value policy of guaranteed issue insurance at age 35 costs $4,050, *but* the first year the death benefit is only $15,000, or one-sixth of the face value. Not until the fifth year does the policy pay the face value. To assure your survivors of $100,000 should you die in the first year, therefore, you would have to buy 6.67 times the face value and pay 6.67 times the premium, or $27,013. The only company I know that writes this kind of insurance, Presidential Life Insurance Company in Nyack, New York, unfortunately sets the maximum at $250,000.

The next most expensive form of insurance is *endowment,* which you don't have to die to get. You recall that the 25-year-old nonsmoking woman could buy $100,000 worth of insurance for $106. Well, the annual premium of a $100,000 endowment, maturing in twenty years, at the age of 25, would cost more than $4,000 (No. 19). That's a 2 percent return! If you'd like your endowment at age 65, and you're 45 now, the annual premium will cost you $4,670 up.

If you want to buy an endowment policy—and millions of people do buy them—you will have no trouble finding a company to write it. Call any agency in town and go to the door and wait for the salesman to show up.

But if you die tomorrow, which is the only reason to buy insurance in the first place, what you will get for that premium is the same as you would get if you bought the lowest cost term—the face value of the policy.

Other more expensive types of insurance include those that you pay off in a certain number of years, such as twenty-payment life (No. 18). This type of insurance does not pay you the full amount while you're still alive, as does endowment, but after the specified number of years you're through paying premiums, and the insurance remains in force until you die. It has a cash surrender value.

If you like to work out complex puzzles, or enjoy being in a state of total confusion, you can find special plans offered in great variety by all the big companies. You can find plans with a mishmash of everything—endowment, provisions for spouse and children, combinations of permanent and term, bearing all kinds of fancy names.

I did not put this kind of insurance on the table because the plans cost you just about any amount the salesman can get out of you. As a matter of fact, to repeat it again, that's what the insurance salesman sells—whatever he can get you to pay for.

Now let's compare costs of term insurance policies.

I was talking to a fellow at a cocktail party the other night. He's thirty-five, owns his own computer business, and thinks he's sharp as a tack. He told me he had figured the insurance business out, cashed in his whole life policy, and bought term. He said, with a smug look on his face, that he had to threaten to go to another agent to get it.

I can talk frankly to people now. "Sounds like you drove a good bargain," I said. "Let's see, I know you're in good shape and don't smoke. You probably paid about two bucks a thousand, huh?"

His jaw dropped down to his kneecaps. He wouldn't tell me how much he paid, but he told me the company. I looked the rates up in *Best's*—$5.08 per thousand! That's my smart computer friend. He paid $508 for $100,000 worth of term insurance. Look at the comparison table and you'll see what he could have gotten it for if he'd been as smart as he thinks he is.

Term insurance is available from a wide variety of sources. You can buy it from a salesman, if you can make him sell it to you. You can buy it through a group. In Massachusetts,

New York, and Connecticut you can buy it from a savings bank. You can buy it by mail. Whichever method you choose, there are high premiums and low premiums.

Many persons in America today have group insurance where they work. Some companies even pay the premiums. It would be silly not to take the paid insurance, of course. But with plans in which the employee pays, the premium may be low or it may be high. What's low? What's high? This is what I am telling you in this chapter.

To get a fix on term insurance, let's start with the lowest cost premiums. When I was talking with Mike Lynch, who as leader of the Federal Trade Commission task force on life insurance should certainly be one of the most knowledgeable insurance experts in the country, I asked him about his insurance. He said he bought it through his professional society, the American Statistical Association. The ASA referred me to Smith, Sternau Organization, Inc., a full-service administration house in Washington, D.C. It administers insurance for more than a hundred organizations, using several insurance companies. ASA policies are written by New York Life Insurance Company.

A 35-year-old member of the American Statistical Association can buy, by mail, $100,000 worth of insurance for $266. New York Life is a mutual company, and pays dividends. To members of the ASA, it has not only been paying 50 percent dividends, but paying them at the end of the first year. So the premium amounts to $133 (No. 1).

Actually, of course, taking the time value of money into consideration, the company has had the use of the entire premium for a year, and the insured has not. New York Life's net yield on invested assets was 7.43 percent in 1979, which added to $266 is $286. Thus we could say the premium is really $133 plus 7.43 per cent of $266, or $153. Few people would figure their personal accounts that close; even so, it's a good price and an easy way to buy insurance.

Unfortunately for those of us who would like to buy our

insurance so easily and cheaply, we can't all belong to the American Statistical Association. However, when we set out to buy our own insurance, we can look at the ASA rates as something to dream on. I have listed them, net, in the comparison table. If you belong to some group that offers insurance, check the ASA rates for comparison.

Incidentally, although I recommend non-participating insurance in most individual cases, I can see the reason for participating insurance in these group arrangements. Naturally, members of the group want low-cost insurance. Smith, Sternau, acting as a third party, negotiates the rates, based on the mortality rates of the group over the years. Statisticians, to single out one group, have a very favorable mortality rate. Dynamiters do not.

But suppose, en route to their convention, a planeload of statisticians goes down. That would result in a heavy financial loss. So by paying a larger amount at the beginning of the year, the group provides a buffer for the company against catastrophe and maintains a stable program.

Another good buy in insurance today is available to the millions of persons in the world of education. The Teachers' Insurance and Annuity Association (TIAA) of New York was set up by philanthropists for the sole purpose of providing insurance at a fair cost to the nations' teachers. It is a stock company, but under its charter it distributes its profits to its policyholders each year.

Again using a 35-year-old male, $100,000 worth of insurance purchased from TIAA (No. 5) would cost $373, of which 47.98 percent, or $179, would be returned at the end of the year, for a net premium of $194. This is a five-year term policy, which means that the premium stays the same for five years. For anybody connected with an educational institution, this is a good deal. As with the ASA, you don't have to try to find someone who will sell you a low-cost policy. Just call (800) 223-1200, and they'll take care of you.

As for me, I prefer to pay the lower non-participating

premium, as opposed to the higher initial premium with eventual return of dividend, at the beginning of the year, and use the difference right now.

Another large group of persons eligible for low-cost term insurance is composed of the people who live in Massachusetts. There, $100,000 in the Massachusetts Savings Bank Life Insurance (SBLI) special nonsmokers' policy would cost $168 (No. 7) for a 35-year-old. (Actually, $50,000 is the maximum available.) One of the advantages of SBLI is that you can simply walk into any savings bank and buy it without being hassled and importuned to buy something more expensive. New York (No. 12) and Connecticut sell SBLI in lower amounts at higher prices.

Another easy way to buy insurance is through your credit card. Wouldn't you think this would be an efficient and cost-saving way of buying insurance? The insurance company has a group of prospects that have already been screened, it saves the commission it pays its agents to bring in individual accounts, and it turns the collecting over to the credit card people. But again, in comparison to a $117 premium for a policy for a 35-year-old bought in the usual way with a commission to agent and broker, the premiums for $100,000 are: Shell Oil (No. 9), $282; American Express (No. 10), $276; and Visa (No. 11), $297. (These figures are projections from the maximum amounts of insurance available.)

There are other ways you can buy insurance by mail or by telephone. Surely every football fan has seen Roger Staubach peddling mail order insurance to veterans in TV commercials during the Super Bowl game. I called the number, (800) 523-0378, and received a bunch of information and a membership card with my name and number embossed in gold. The premium, projected from the maximum available, would be $354 for $100,000.

This policy is written by the National Home Life Assurance Company of Pennsylvania, which also writes the policies for Shell credit card holders. As you can see, you pay more if you buy it through Roger.

Suppose a National Home agent comes out and sells it to you? Then it would be $221, or $133 less.

Sometimes in life it is the nicest people, the people who can least afford it, who pay the most. Think of all the young couples who respond to the Gerber Life Insurance Company's mail order appeal. I saw this insert, featuring a full-color comic strip, in a Sunday paper. It's tied in with Gerber baby food, and there are pictures of babies and children all over it. The advertising copy tugs at both your heartstrings and your pocketbook. It repeats over and over that this is low-cost insurance, as if repeating it will make it so.

But it isn't so. This is very high-cost insurance.

On the front page of the insert, next to the comic strip, is a caption: "Will you give up one lunch a month for your loved ones? $10,000 life insurance for as little as $4.84 a month (man aged 26)." Well, $10,000 life insurance for as little as $4.84 a month comes out to $5.81 per thousand of life insurance, which is a lot to pay, even for a 26-year-old fellow who eats $4.84 lunches.

The maximum amount offered in this comic strip solicitation is $20,000. Let's see what our 35-year-old guinea pig would pay Gerber (No. 14). Monthly payments for $20,000 are $13.52, or $162.24 per year. That's $8.11 per thousand —at that rate I'd be paying Gerber $811 for the same amount of insurance I get for $117!

The Gerber policy is unusual in that it is a twenty-year term policy; the premiums remain the same for twenty years. That means that these nice young couples pay more at the beginning, when they are less likely to have it to pay.

Yet the life insurance industry is so confusing and so little is known about its rates, so ignorant and trusting are the people who purchase these high-cost policies and support the industry, that Gerber and other purveyors of high-cost insurance sell a lot of it to those unfortunate couples who can least afford the high prices. Between 1974 and 1979 Gerber doubled the amount of life insurance they have in force.

It's not only open season on the people who respond to comic strip advertisements. College graduates also provide some happy hunting for insurance salesmen, and gullible alumni directors often act as native guides. So I asked three friends who went to big universities to check their alumni associations. They are from the University of Michigan, the University of Virginia, and the University of Missouri.

The Michigan alumnus received a large four-color brochure, including scenic views of Ann Arbor, with a description of the "group term life insurance protection program." Under the heading *May we anticipate your questions?* is the following:

Q. How about the cost . . . Are the premiums really low?
A. Yes. Group insurance costs the buyer much less than if purchased outside of a group. Plus, there are additional savings accomplished through the economies of mass merchandising and reduction in sales costs.

I'll tell you how "really low" these premiums really are. The maximum amount you can buy is $75,000. At age 30–39, the really low semiannual premium is $106.13, $212.26 per year, or $2.83 per thousand. Projected to $100,000, that's $283 for the amount of insurance I would get for $117.

The Virginia alumnus had a lot more fun. He was referred by his alumni association to an 800 number, and wound up talking to a pleasant voice in Corpus Christi, Texas. Soon the mail brought a Special Bulletin from the University of Virginia Alumni Association, over the signature of Gilbert J. Sullivan, director of alumni, advising "alumni and their spouses of their right to apply for high-limit term insurance at exceptionally attractive rates through the Trust of the Alumni Group Insurance Plan."

What does it cost? Well, the 35-year-old Virginia alumnus can buy $100,000 worth of insurance for $29.50 a month, an annual total of $354. So that "exceptionally attractive" rate is three times what can be purchased elsewhere.

The Missouri alumnus wound up with the University of Missouri-Kansas City Alumni Association Life Insurance Plan. It is identical to the Virginia plan, except that it is Keith G. Grafing, president of the alumni association, who talks of the exceptionally attractive rates.

All three policies require alumni association membership, which means you have to pay dues, too. And all three are written by the Northwestern National Life Insurance Company.

Want to have some fun? Check with the alumni association of your own college and see what happens. Maybe you, too, can get some of those exceptionally attractive rates.

Such is the ingenuity of the insurance industry that it can come up with a high-cost term policy, a low-cost permanent policy.

Several companies now offer the high-cost term policy, *deposit term,* which I discussed earlier. Here's how the Fireman's Fund American Life Insurance Company works it. At age 35, for a $100,000 policy, the basic premium for the first year is $248. The additional first year premium, a one-time payment, is $400, total $648 (No. 15). The basic premium increases each year. At the end of the tenth year, if you're still paying, your original additional premium becomes a cash value of double the amount, $800. You can borrow it! Deposit term is high-cost term insurance.

First Colony Life Insurance Company has a policy that's low-cost permanent insurance. At age 35 a $100,000 policy only costs $143 (No. 6). Permanent or term, that's a bargain! The catch is that cash values are practically nonexistent for the first twenty years, and then the premium rises sharply. So what. My philosophy is to buy the lowest cost insurance available, year by year. When your policy is no longer the lowest cost, buy something else. If at that time you are uninsurable and stuck with that policy, you are still no worse off.

And now you have an idea of what you can get it for.

Chapter 11

Your Misfortune
Is My Opportunity

One morning in July, 1981, I was having breakfast and watching the *Today* show when I suddenly found myself listening to grown men arguing about whether you should borrow money on your insurance. I was surprised that anybody could get five minutes of dialogue out of so elementary a question.

I remembered a day a few years before . . .

"There's a woman on the phone and she sounds like she's crying," my secretary said. "She wants information on how to borrow on an insurance policy."

"Thanks," I said. It would have been a simple matter for her to mail the caller a form to fill out, but she had followed the correct office procedure in referring the call to me.

The woman on the other end of the line was indeed close to tears. She was calling from a motel. She and her husband were from California. They had three children. They had come all the way across the continent to take a splendid opportunity with a new company here in the East, using their savings for the move. Now the company was out of business and her husband was out of a job. She sounded pitiful.

"We have an insurance policy with your company," she said. "My husband got it ten years ago. He's out trying to find another position, and he asked me to call the company office here and find out if we can borrow on the policy. When we first got it the agent said we could."

Ten years. Hmmmm, I thought. "May I ask how much the policy is for? Look where it says Face Amount in the little window."

"Fifty thousand dollars. Do you think . . . ?"

"I think we may be able to work something out."

"Oh, that's wonderful," she said. "May I come to your office and pick up whatever it is we need?"

"I wouldn't think of making you come to us," I said. "I'll be glad to come and take a look at your policy, and I'll bring everything that's necessary to make a loan in case you do have some cash value. When will your husband be back? It would be better to see you both together."

We made the appointment for that night. I wasn't about to let her come to the office. In the insurance business we go to you. We want to see where you live, how you live, everything about you.

Especially when *you* call *us.* Especially when you already have a policy—you've been softened up. Especially when you want to borrow money on it. You think that this makes you a less promising prospect? Not at all. *Any* change in your life, for better or worse, makes you a prospect. I will come to you, look over the situation, and if I am any good at all in this business, I will find a way to make my visit worthwhile.

When I knocked on the door that night they opened it almost immediately. They'd been waiting. They told me the whole story all over again, she nearly in a panic, he obviously very, very worried. I looked at their policy. Eureka. They had a cash value of almost $10,000.

At times like this I was proud to be an insurance agent. I could help these people.

"It's going to work out okay," I said. "You'll look back on this as an adventure someday." Then I groaned and looked serious. "But there's one thing that worries me."

"What's that?" they asked. They had confidence in me now. If something worried me, they wanted to know about it.

"I'm concerned about the protection you will lose in borrowing against your insurance," I said. "Here you are all the way across the country, three thousand miles from home. This policy has proven to be a godsend, but I hate to see you deplete it. If anything should happen to you, God forbid, your wife and the kids would have a rough go of it." I shook my head sadly. So did they.

"But what can we do?" he asked.

"I would recommend increasing the policy," I said. "By at least the amount you are taking out of it. As a matter of fact, costs have gone up since you acquired that policy, and it would probably be prudent to increase it anyway. In a few short years you will have built the cash value up again, and in the meantime you will know that your family is protected."

"But how can I increase the policy when I have to borrow from it just to meet day-to-day expenses?" he said. "I'm going to have a tough enough time paying the premium when it's due."

"I think you ought to take that worry off your shoulders, and pay the premium out of the loan," I said. "Now let me see, how much do you think your survivors would need if, God forbid . . . ?"

So we increased his insurance by $25,000. They were very grateful both for my help and my confidence in him as shown by my faith that he would pay the increased premiums. He paid the first year's premium in full out of the money he had borrowed.

I was glad, of course, to fulfill my obligations as a life insurance agent.

And my commission was a little over $290.

That kind of thing happened many times. I sold a lot of high-priced insurance (it wouldn't pay to sell any other kind) to people who had to borrow to buy it. It was easy, as a matter of fact. Insurance is sold on emotion, and there's no emotion like being so broke you have to borrow on your insurance. The industry trains its salesmen to take advantage of the opportunity.

Suppose you're *not* broke. Should you borrow on your insurance then? That was the question on the *Today* show. And now I was no longer a life insurance salesman, but a consumer-oriented *ex*-salesman.

Of course you should borrow on it, every last nickel, unless it makes more sense to cash it in. Anybody who has not already borrowed to the hilt on his permanent life insurance is simply compounding the mistake he made when he bought it in the first place. There's at least a billion dollars sitting there waiting for all you holders of cash value insurance. Go get it.

Yet the industry spokesman, Robert Waldron of the American Council of Life Insurance, not only advised against borrowing on your policy but said that the money is not really yours to borrow. It should be left in the company's hands so the company can continue to invest it.

Even after all these years I sometimes shake my head in amazement at what industry spokesmen say, and how other people just sit there and accept it. How in the world can the cash value in your insurance policy not be yours? This is the way the industry designed cash value insurance, this is what the salesman was trained to say, and this is how he sold it. I couldn't estimate how many times I've told some confused blue-collar worker, or prosperous businessman for that matter: "Now, sir, in this column you will see how your cash value mounts up. Look, at this point you will see that your cash value is more than the total amount of premiums you have paid!"

And then, depending on the customer, I would tell him what he could do with the money—make a down payment on a home, put the kids through college, augment his retirement fund, or use it for an emergency.

As it stood in July 1981, policyholders had borrowed more than $44 billion from their own cash value, paying the industry interest on it. Some of these people used it to pay their premiums under the terms of the minimum deposit arrangement their companies set up for them. Some needed the money for some purpose they deemed worthwhile, and got it, just the way the salesman told them they could.

But some—and this is what really bugs the insurance industry—have borrowed the money for another purpose altogether. They have taken it out, paying 4 to 8 percent on it as was originally specified by the company, and invested that money at much higher interest rates. In July 1981 you could open the financial section of any large newspaper and see virtually riskless opportunities paying 12 to 18 percent, and other ventures offering the more daring even higher potential.

If you could get that much interest, you'd have to pay even more to borrow money. So guess who found themselves having to borrow money at 10, 14, and 18 percent in order to lend it out at half that? That's right, the insurance companies.

Does your heart bleed for them? Mine doesn't. I remember too well sending out a hundred form letters a week telling people that through life insurance they could build up a nest egg they could borrow on. I remember being driven and rewarded to sell that insurance, and as a manager driving others to sell it. The whole industry was pushing it. So now they have to deliver just exactly what they said.

If you still have any doubt about borrowing your cash value, I know someone who can resolve the issue for you—

any eight-year-old kid who has passed second grade arithmetic. Check the interest rate on your policy, the interest rate being paid by your savings bank or money market fund, and ask the second grade student to subtract one from the other. That is what you are losing, and that is what you stand to gain.

As for the postulation that borrowing the cash value reduces the face value of the policy, this is only true if you fritter the money away. If you invest it, you are increasing the death benefit.

The industry cannot change the rate of interest on the policy you now have. It is, however, lobbying for legislation setting a higher rate of interest in future policies. Several states have already gone along with this, and more probably will. Remember that most state legislatures do what the insurance industry tells them to do. This means that those persons buying whole life, or cash value policies, in those states from now on will have to pay more to borrow back their own money from the insurance companies. It certainly makes sense for the insurance industry to do this, but it doesn't make sense for you to buy that kind of policy.

For now, let's say you have cash value in your life insurance and you wish to borrow it. What do you do?

First of all, you must realize that the company doesn't want to lend it to you. The interest you will pay may be as low as 5 or 6 percent. What do you think the company is getting for that money now?

So you can be sure that when you call your agent or the local office of the company, it's not going to be easy. All you need is a form to fill out, and the office has plenty of them, but the girl who answers the phone isn't going to send you one. She's got orders to move you up to higher authority.

Whoever that may be, manager or salesman, is supposed to try first to dissuade you from borrowing the money at all. He may convince you that everything is going to be all right, or he may make the very idea of borrowing on your insurance so terrible that you are ashamed to go through with it. Or, number two on the company's list of preferences, you may be told to take your policy to the bank and use it as collateral for a bank loan. Some people actually do, paying three times as much interest to the bank as they would to the insurance company for their own cash value.

But from the salesman's point of view, we don't get a penny for conserving money for the company. Salesmen make their money selling insurance, and a person seeking to borrow money is a prospect. Your misfortune may be my opportunity to sell you more insurance. Whatever it is, we will try somehow to twist it into a reason for you to buy more insurance.

It is amazing to me that people don't realize this. How can people who want to borrow money honestly believe that an insurance salesman is going to hurry through dinner, or maybe miss it altogether, burn up gasoline driving to their house, and sit and visit and listen to their hard-luck story, which he has heard a hundred times before, solely to deliver, out of the kindness of his heart, a printed form? And then point out to them a figure, printed in black and white on their own insurance policy. Confusing as insurance policies may be, there are a few things that are plain to see. One is the face value of the policy, another is the cash value, increasing year by year. Sometimes it's in units of a thousand, sometimes it represents the total value. You look at the number of years the policy is in force and follow the line across to the cash value.

It is there. It is yours. *Take it.* First, insist that the agency mail you a form, or drop into the office and pick it up yourself. If a salesman does bring it to you, accept his help and say thanks, but say no thanks when he tries to sell you more expensive insurance. Don't feel sorry for him. He may not sell you tonight, but he'll make up for it with somebody else tomorrow.

Chapter 12

Four Tales of Insurance

Paul and Pam

When a young woman I know heard about this project, she sneaked her husband's insurance policies out of his desk drawer and asked me to take a look at them.

They had been fighting over these two $10,000 policies for months. The premiums amounted to $375 a year. She thought they were a waste of money.

They do not have children, but they hope to someday. The husband, Paul, is a dentist, thirty-seven. The wife, Pam, is younger and a teacher. They've paid off their mortgage.

Paul had bought the first policy long before they were married. His father had died when he was a boy. When he was eighteen and went off to college, a friend of the family who was an insurance agent came by and, supported by Paul's mother, sold him a $10,000 life insurance policy with his mother as beneficiary. That way Paul could go off to school comfortable in the knowledge that someone would take care of his mother if anything happened to him.

The salesman happened to represent a mutual company, so what Paul bought was a $10,000 participating whole life policy. It would pay dividends. What does an eighteen-year-old know about such things? He was talked out of the only immediately available value in the policy—the dividends. Instead of being used to reduce the premium, the dividends would go back to the company to buy additional paid-up insurance. The premium was $178, which paid the agent at least 55 percent, or $97.90 the first year, with renewals thereafter. Easy money.

It was even easier six years later. Paul, now twenty-four, married to Pam and about to go into the service, was ripe for another $10,000 policy: premiums $197, commission of at least $108 plus renewals. Paul has been paying on these two policies ever since. The salesman has been collecting his renewals ever since.

Here's what the policies look like today:

Policy #1:		
Face Value		$10,000
Paid Up Additions from Dividends		2,120
Total Insurance		$12,120
Cash Value		$ 2,080
Additional Cash Value		921
Total Cash Value		$ 3,001
Annual Premium		$ 178

Policy #2:		
Face Value		$10,000
Paid Up Additions		1,041
Total Insurance		$11,041
Cash Value		$ 1,570
Additional Cash Value		452
Total Cash Value		$ 2,022
Annual Premium		$ 197

Total of two policies: Total Insurance $23,161
Total Cash Value $ 5,023

Total Annual Premiums $ 375

First of all, did he need either policy when he bought them? His mother was apparently able to do without the first when he got married. His wife was perfectly healthy and capable, and she didn't want either.

And if he needed insurance at all, did he need $10,000, $20,000, or $23,000—or was that what the salesman figured he was good for?

Did he need those expensive, permanent policies? For half as much money he could have purchased five times the insurance.

Did he need to start saving for the future? This was one hell of an expensive way to do it. If he'd started investing the premiums for the first policy, $178, at 6 percent fifteen years ago, when he bought it, he'd have $4,400 of his own by now, not $3,000 "cash value" doing him no good whatever. The premiums for the second policy, $197, would have produced over $3,500, total $7,900.

But that's past history now. Instead of figuring what might have been, let's see what he can do with what he's got.

Although he'd have a lot more if he'd put those premiums away at compound interest over the years, he does have a total cash value in the two policies of just over $5,000. That's money working for the company, not for Paul. By not using it, he is losing the income he could get from it.

Of course, Paul, being a good middle-class American boy, will be shocked at the idea of borrowing his cash value, or worse, cashing the policies in. But maybe some figures will stifle his screams.

First, let's consider borrowing it. The policies specify that he can do so, at 5 percent interest. When Pam came to me, the local savings and loan associations were advertising rates of 16.55 percent for an effective interest of 18.27 on minimum accounts of $100 held for two and a half years. This figure may seem high or low on the day you read this. The fact remains that if they had invested their money then, it would still be receiving that rate. So let us say that he does indeed borrow it at 5 percent and invest it at 18.27.

$$\$5,000 \times 18.27\% = \$914 \text{ (investment income)}$$
$$\text{less } \$5,000 \times 5\% = \underline{\$250} \text{ (interest due insurance)}$$
$$\text{equals} \$664 \text{ (net annual income)}$$

The premiums, you recall, total $375 a year. So if Paul borrows the cash value and invests it with his local savings and loan, he will be able to pay his premiums—and pocket $289 a year before taxes!

I know what his first protest will be. He will say that borrowing the cash value reduces his insurance.

And I will say that this is indeed true. It does reduce his insurance. But it does not reduce the amount that he leaves Pam. Borrowing $5,000 reduces the face amount of $23,000 to $18,000. But that $5,000 is in the savings bank earning money for him instead of for the insurance company. It still goes to Pam if Paul dies.

Actually it keeps on rising because of the dividend option Paul checked off twenty years ago. Here was another recommendation I had for Pam, whether they borrowed the cash value or kept the policies as they were. Paul's dividends had bought him a few thousand dollars more of insurance—but they could have been used all these years to reduce the premiums. This would be the simplest, most conservative step Paul and Pam could take.

I got her to look for the past payment requests. They showed that one policy earned a dividend of $100, the other $73. By using these to reduce the premiums, 375 − 173 = 202, they would reduce their annual payment to $202.

Of course, he could use both the dividends *and* the income

from the cash value. Then, instead of paying out $375 a year, plus lost interest, he would have $462 *and* his precious policies, not to mention a happier Pam. But that might be a little too much for Paul. You're not supposed to have your cake and eat it too.

I don't believe that there is any possibility of Paul's cashing in his policies. Rather, he will cling to them like teddy bears. Nevertheless, let's work out what will happen if he cashes in, takes his $5,000, and runs.

Of course, if Paul and Pam take the money out and blow it, they will indeed wipe out the amount of death protection. They are smart enough to know that, and they won't do it.

So let's say they cash in the policies and invest the $5,000 at the effective annual yield of 18.27 percent. They will again get $914 a year, but now he won't have to deduct the $250 paid to the company.

What can he do with $914, or whatever he has after taxes? (I don't know what bracket he's in.) For one thing, he can buy insurance. Only this time, let's do it intelligently.

First, Paul must answer an important question, the question he should have asked himself at age eighteen when he bought the first policy, at age twenty-four when he bought the second, and every year since then, as a matter of fact. What do they *need* in the way of insurance?

We are going to discuss that question in Chapter 15. They will have to work out their own program like everybody else. The children they don't have, but want, complicate things. Should they pay out money now for an eventuality yet to occur? How much? My advice is not to buy insurance for children you don't have.

With or without children, Paul would want to provide some protection for Pam. If and when they have children, he can increase it.

When they decide how much they want, I will advise them on how to buy it.

As it stands now, he is paying $375 a year and losing $914

a year in the interest he does not collect on the cash value. That's a total of $1,289 going out the window. For that he has $23,000 worth of insurance.

For that I could sell him $1,000,000 in annual renewable term insurance. Or, for less than $200, I could sell him a $100,000 policy, and he will have the difference of a thousand bucks or so, after taxes, to invest. The premium would increase each year, but so would the return on his investment. He'd be better off.

Another possibility is a five-year renewable term plan, for during that time their family plans will probably materialize.

I'd like to talk with Paul and Pam further, after they have a good long talk between themselves, to learn what they really need and want in the way of insurance, and to help them get it.

But one thing's for sure. They can do a lot better than $1,289 a year for a measly $23,000 in whole life insurance.

Joanie

I'm sitting here looking at a pathetic little document, one of millions filed away in homes all across the country. It's an insurance policy for $2,000. A fiction writer could base a novel on it. It belongs to a friend of mine named Joanie. That's not her name, but the story is real and the figures are exact.

In 1944 she was twenty-one years old, one of five brothers and sisters of an Irish Catholic lace-curtain family living in Newark. Two of the boys were in the armed services. Joanie trudged bravely off to work each morning, contributing her bit to the family, to the war effort, to all the good American things.

So when the life insurance salesman came by on New Year's Day to offer her the opportunity to have an insurance policy of her very own, she was pleased and flattered. The family gathered round the dining-room table, where the kids had always done their homework and all family affairs were talked over, and they discussed a Life Insurance Policy for Joanie. They all gave her lots of advice, but as is obvious from the policy, nobody knew any more about it than she did.

What she wound up with was a $2,000 policy, twenty-payment life, $5.40 a month. The salesman would come by to collect on the first day of every month, along with other premiums in the household.

We don't need a calculator to see that that totals $64.80 per year, or $32.40 per thousand of life insurance. The price of insurance across the board may have been higher then, but by any yardstick, any time, $32.40 per thousand was a disgraceful amount to pay.

But Joanie paid it. Or *somebody* paid it when she wasn't home when the agent dropped by, or when she was home but she didn't have any money. The brothers came back from the war, and for years the family lived happily together and paid each other's insurance premiums. It became a monthly habit. A knock on the door, "There's Mister What's His Name!" and everybody would run around scrounging up the premiums.

Joanie got married and moved out, forgetting all about the policy. The agent didn't; he came around every month to collect and every month somebody paid. Finally it was paid up. The total paid in was $1,295. If Joanie had invested that amount at the savings and loan, or even in war bonds, she'd have had a lot more than $1,295. As it was, what she had was a life insurance policy for $2,000, with her mother as beneficiary, and $974 in cash value, which the company would lend her back at 5 percent interest. At the time, 5 percent was no bargain.

Also involved was the accumulated value of dividends, which had been applied to the purchase of paid-up additions to the face value. However, these dividends had been long since forgotten.

So had the policy, as far as Joanie was concerned. She was living her own life, 500 miles away, with a husband and children and a home and lots of bills, including her husband's insurance. It wasn't until after her mother's death that the policy came to light. It also came to light that some of the cash value had been borrowed. Joanie remembered it vaguely, for she'd had to sign a paper, but it was something one of the older brothers back home had asked her to do, and like a dutiful little sister, she had done it.

How much was borrowed, and when, Joanie doesn't remember. Stuck in the policy, however, is a notice from the company, dated January 1, 1973, to the effect that the amount of principal was $610.31, and the amount of interest due was $32.49.

"I think I'd made a payment before that, though," Joanie said. "I remember resolving that I would pay it all up, and when I died my husband and the children would have something to remember me by. I really determined to do it. Oh, yes, I'd called the local office of the company, and the man there said that was a good thing to do."

Let's see now, what was the financial situation then? The face value was $2,000, the borrowed amount $610.31, the amount of interest due $32.49. She thus had $1,389.69 worth of insurance in force. Or, to put it another way, she was paying $32.49 for $1,389.69 worth of insurance, term insurance. That's $23 per thousand.

Joanie's plans, however, were relegated to the folder stuck away in a drawer containing all the family's insurance papers. Her husband said he'd take care of it. He didn't know any more about insurance than she did, however—I've seen his portfolio and it's a mess. Other bills seemed to have higher priority, and he didn't get around to paying the interest, and the interest was added to the principal, and year by year it mounted up.

When I looked at it in 1981 the principal amounted to $1,190.15, on which the interest was $59.51. The face value of the policy, $2,000 less $1,190.15, was now $809.85. She was now paying sixty bucks for less than $1,000 of insurance.

She was also losing whatever she could have earned on that $800, but of course she never thought of that.

According to the table of values, her cash value is going up at the rate of $24 a year. But the interest she owes is more than twice that, and it's compounding. Thus, in two years the cash value will be less than the principal of the loan.

And the policy will eventually self-destruct.

And I think of the number of times over the years the agent came to the door to collect, and somebody scraped up $5.40 a month for sister's insurance policy. It was worth so much then, so little now.

What can Joanie do? What should she have done? What should all the rest of you out there do, with policies stuck away in drawers gathering dust and losing interest?

Okay, what Joanie can do right now is determine the total cash value of the policy. That requires writing to the company and asking for the information on dividends. The address of the company is on the policy.

The letter looks like this:

Date_____

Name of insured _____ Policy Number_____
Please let me know the total cash value, including dividends, on the above policy.

The answer: The cash value was $1,346, additional cash value from dividends $525.39, plus terminal dividend of $140 —total $2,011.39. But the loan was now up to $1,190.15 plus interest of $58.17—total $1,248.32. Joanie had $763.07 coming.

"Take it," I said.

She did. She could have written the home office again, but it happened that the company had an office in town. She went by one morning, and in two weeks she received a check. She deposited it in a money market fund, and instead of eating up Joanie's money at 5 percent, it is today producing the current rate of interest. With it Joanie can buy more insurance, for final expenses, than she had.

What should she have done at the very beginning, when she first learned she had a policy with a loan on it? I think she should have done the same thing. We have seen that to pay the interest was the equivalent of paying an exorbitant amount all over again for insurance she had already paid an exorbitant amount for before. Including the dividends, which she didn't even know about, there was some value left in the policy. Take it.

If there had been no loan on the policy, all the more reason she should have taken the cash value. She was losing the interest it was drawing for somebody else. She could have been getting it for herself and her family all along.

Joe

It is hard not to be annoyed sometimes by people who trust their friends to do their thinking for them in matters for which they should be responsible.

I know a fellow named Joe. He's a good ol' boy, with lots of friends. He is good at what he does, but what he does has nothing to do with finances. He would give a friend the shirt off his back or honest advice in his own area, and in his own trusting way he expects his friends to treat him the same way.

That's all very fine, except when he is dealing with the security of his family. And when his friend is a life insurance salesman.

Back in 1952, when Joe was thirty-six years old, with a wife and child, he realized that his $10,000 Veterans Administration life insurance policy would hardly provide for his wife and child if he should die. Maybe he had a nudge in that direction from one of his good friends, a life insurance salesman.

His concern for his survivors was certainly laudable. His next course of action was not. Like so many people in that situation, people unsophisticated in the realm of family economics, he did not even know how to begin research into what he should do next. So there was his friend, the life insurance salesman, the man he played tennis with on Saturdays and had lunch with on Tuesdays.

And his friend, of course, like me and a few hundred thousand other insurance peddlers, said, "You came to the right person. I am a professional. I will advise you on this important matter."

Ridiculous! He sold Joe a life insurance policy: $10,000, premium $216.80, payable until he died. Permanent insurance, non-participating, $21.68 per thousand. I'd say that Joe's friend got at least $125, probably more, that first year, and he is still drawing a few dollars on it today.

So we come on down through the years, and now good old Joe has a new friend, me. He is now sixty-five. His children are grown and taking care of themselves. His house is paid for. He's making a living, such as it is. But he has found other things to do with his money over the years than to invest it, so his wife isn't going to get very much when he dies. She still has a few years to go before Social Security.

And Joe is still paying away on his insurance policy, so that his wife will have it when he is gone. Now let's see. What has he got, and what is it costing him?

Well, what he's got is what he always had: $10,000 if he dies, no more, no less. And he's paying out $216.80 a year for it, just as he has been doing for almost thirty years. That's what Joe thinks it costs him.

It actually costs him a lot more, a whole lot more. On the last page of his policy, in the table of surrender and loan values, we see that at age sixty-five, the cash value of this policy is $513.38 per thousand. He can borrow it at 6 percent. (His company wants 1 percent more than Joanie's.) This is the actual current cost of maintaining Joe's policy:

$5,134	Cash value
×18.27%	Current interest rate forfeited
$938.00	Current interest earnings forfeited
+217.00	Current annual premium payable
$1,155.00	Cost to maintain policy *this year*

So it looks like Joe is paying $116 per thousand for his insurance, doesn't it?

Actually, it costs him more than *that*. This cash value is not on top of the death benefit, but is a part of it. If Joe dies tomorrow, his wife is not going to get $10,000 plus the cash value; she is going to get the same $10,000 she would have gotten thirty years ago. Yet the company admits that this $5,134 cash value is Joe's, which means that today it is risking only the difference, $4,866. If Joe takes out his cash value, as he should, he would need to purchase only $4,866 worth of insurance to provide his beneficiary with the $10,000 his policy now provides.

So it costs Joe $1,155 for $4,866 worth of life insurance, or $237 per one thousand dollars.

That is one hell of an expensive insurance policy.

How much has it cost him over the past twenty-eight years? Well, we can multiply the annual premium, $216.80, times twenty-eight, and get a total of $6,070.40. As we have seen, however, that is too simple. Economic ignoramus that he is, the laws of economics nevertheless dictate that Joe must be given credit for the time value of his money. If instead of paying the annual premiums he had invested that amount at 6 percent, he would today have $15,748.31. If he takes out his $5,133.80 cash value, his cost will be $10,615 for his $10,000 insurance policy over the past twenty-eight years.

Just as a matter of curiosity, I pulled out one of my rate cards for a $10,000 annual renewable term policy, compounded the premiums at 6 percent, and reached a total of $5,574. Joe paid $5,041 too much.

With the help of his good friend the life insurance salesman, Joe made an economic mistake twenty-eight years ago, and it got worse every year. It has now magnified itself to the point where it's really pretty shocking. Good ol' boy or not, he was careless and slipshod when it came to spending family money for family protection. For all that money, he never really bought them much protection in the first place. How far would $10,000 go, even in 1952? If he had planned just a little bit more intelligently, he could have bought more insurance for less money.

But let's try to make some constructive suggestions. At least he can do something now. If he hadn't come to me, he'd still be paying more and more for less and less. He has several viable options.

Option 1. He can borrow his own money, $5,134, from the company, paying 6 percent, or $308, for the privilege. We could get into some sticky accounting here, but let's operate on a simple cash flow basis.

As with Paul and Pam, we chose the savings bank's effective yield of 18.27 percent at that time to work with. I punched it out for him on the calculator: 18.27 percent of $5,134 is $938.

"Hey," he said. "That's a good deal. I've got to pay $308 to get it, plus my premium of $217. I can do that in my head. $525. What does the calculator say?"

The calculator showed that $938 minus $525 equals a cash flow of $413.

"In my favor!" Joe said.

Option 2: He can cash in the policy, make an initial deposit of $5,134, and add each year the $217 he would otherwise have paid in annual premiums. Compounded at 10 percent, a conservative figure, this will give him total savings at age sixty-six of $5,886, at sixty-seven $6,713, and so on until age seventy, when he will have $9,726, which is pretty close to the $10,000 he wanted to leave his heirs all the time anyway. If he continues this, incidentally, and there is no reason why he shouldn't, as he looks in pretty good health to me, he'll have $17,000 at age seventy-five, $29,000 at age eighty.

At some point in there he may stop putting in the annual premium of $217, and start taking out to supplement his retirement income.

Option 3: He can stop paying the premiums and have $8,124 in paid-up insurance. He saves $217 a year, but he loses the interest he could be getting on his cash value—and gives up $2,000 in face value.

Option 4: He can stop paying the premiums and have his coverage—for a limited period of time. This is called Extended Term Insurance, and it's found somewhere in the policy along with cash surrender values. On Joe's policy the table stops at the twentieth year. A call to the local office produced the information that he will be insured until he is seventy-seven. As above, with this option he saves $217, but gives up the income on his cash value plus the pro rata value of his cash value, which he is depleting until he dies. Only if Joe is broke and terminally ill is this a good deal.

Option 5: He can cash in the policy, invest his cash value of $5,134, and use the income to buy another insurance policy at a lower rate. He will need $4,866 additionally to provide the original amount of $10,000. I don't know of any companies that write term insurance in $5,000 amounts. He can, however, buy $10,000 additional. Here are two possibilities. The North American Company for Life and Health Insurance writes five-year renewable term to age one hundred. The premium for $10,000 is $449 starting at age sixty-five. First Colony Life Insurance Company writes the same amount for a premium of $346 at sixty-five. With either policy he will have to begin dipping into the principal in his early seventies to pay the premium. At age eighty he will run out completely and owe a premium of $1,303 to North American, $795 to First Colony. You may say this is one weakness of my argument for term insurance. I say, why does Joe want insurance at eighty? Is he sure he's going to live that long? Who is he going to leave it to?

Though Joe appears to be in good health to me, he may be uninsurable. In that case, scratch Option 5.

After I had outlined his options, Joe suddenly started squirming. Then he said, "Uh, Walt . . ."

Oh, my God, I thought. What has he gone and done now?

His face got red. "I just remembered," he said. "I already borrowed on it."

He didn't even remember what he had borrowed the money for! Anyway, he no longer had it.

So we had to figure all this out again. I'll spare you the details, but because a lot of other people have also borrowed on their insurance in years gone by, I'll continue here briefly for their benefit.

First, Joe recalled that he had made the down payment on a car with the insurance money. Okay, he needed the car. He made a lot more with the car than he would have made letting the cash value sit there.

"You did a good thing, Joe," I said.

Then we determined the amount he had previously borrowed, and the cash value he had built up since. It turned out that by drawing it all out and investing it he would receive enough return to pay the interest on both loans, and have some left over to apply to the premium.

There are millions of Joes out there. Their policies may be for hundreds of thousands or for just hundreds. They may have borrowed on their cash value, as Joe did, but more likely the whole thing is just sitting there, untouched, costing those people a lot of money.

Anyone who says it is not actually costing him money, that this is just a paper loss, couldn't be more wrong. Let me put it this way. Suppose you have $10,000 in an account that pays 15 percent, $1,500 per year. You take it out and put it in a straight savings account paying 5 percent, or $500 a year. Don't tell me that's a paper loss. That's a *real* loss. One thousand bucks!

And it's just as real when you let your cash value make money for some insurance company. Get it out and put it to work for you.

You

Paul and Pam, Joanie, and Joe are only some of the millions of people with existing insurance policies—and problems. But most of those millions of people don't know me, and frankly, I don't know of anyone else in the world who will sit down with them and make a real analysis of their policies. Lord knows your insurance salesman is the last man you want to go to.

So what can you do?

These three cases have provided me with enough information to work out a formula by which you can analyze your insurance yourself.

If you have life insurance, get out your policies. Review them one at a time.

What we are going to try to do is chop the policy down to basics: the amount you pay, the amount of death protection you're buying, the amount of cash value, if any, and the actual cost.

On the front page of your policy you will see the face amount of life insurance, or what your survivors get when you die. You will also see the premium you pay for the face amount. You may also see figures for *double indemnity* or *accidental death, waiver of premium, guaranteed issue, cost of living, optional term coverage, dismemberment.* Ignore them. All these are extras.

If you have a participating policy, you have to get the

amount of your dividend from your last year's bill and subtract it from your premium to get the net payment.

Annualize the premium. If it is paid by the month, multiply by twelve. If quarterly, by four.

Divide the premium by the number of thousands of the face amount. The result is the premium per thousand of your life insurance, which you can compare to the table in Chapter 10.

If you have term insurance, you're lucky. You can stop right here.

But if you are one of the policyholders of two and a half trillions of dollars in permanent life insurance in force today, read on.

What does your insurance actually cost you today? With my formula you can determine this cost. If you have permanent insurance, this will be the most important form in this book to you. I call it How To Calculate Cost of Current Death Benefit. Or, how much you pay today for the money your survivors will get if you die tomorrow.

You may be paying a lot more than you think.

Here is how to fill in the form. First, determine the amount of total cash available. You get this figure from the table in the policy. Most policies express this figure in amount per thousand, so make sure you multiply the amount by the number of thousands of dollars given on the face of the policy. Enter the amount of total cash value on Line 1.

Next, have you borrowed on your policy? If you have not borrowed, enter the amount from Line 1 onto Line 5. If you have, and you do not remember the exact amount or the rate of interest you pay the insurance company, you may call the agency or home office and get the amount. Enter the amount borrowed on Line 2 and the rate of interest on Line 3. Multiply Line 2 by Line 3 and enter the result on Line 4. This is the amount in dollars you are paying for the borrowed money.

If Line 2 is less than Line 1 (if you have borrowed less than the full cash value), deduct the amount borrowed

HOW TO CALCULATE COST OF CURRENT DEATH BENEFIT

1. $＿＿＿＿ Total cash value

2. $＿＿＿＿ Cash value borrowed to date

3. ＿＿＿% Interest rate charged by insurance company

4. $＿＿＿＿ Cost (line 2 × line 3)

5. $＿＿＿＿ Cash value not borrowed

6. ＿＿＿% Interest rate you could be earning

7. $＿＿＿＿ Cost (earnings forfeited, line 5 × line 6)

8. $＿＿＿＿ Net annualized premium

9. $＿＿＿＿ Total cost to maintain policy this year (line 4 + line 7 + line 8)

10. $＿＿＿＿ Face amount of policy

11. $＿＿＿＿ Total cash value (from line 1)

12. $＿＿＿＿ Death benefit at risk (line 10 − line 11)

13. ＿＿＿＿ Death benefit at risk expressed as unit per thousand dollars (line 12, decimal moved three places to left)

14. $＿＿＿＿ Cost per $1,000 (line 9 ÷ line 13)

(Line 2) from the total (Line 1) and enter on Line 5. Line 6 is the rate of interest available at the time you are reading this. You will have to assume what this rate is. If you are a sophisticated investor, you will have no problem. If you are unsure, call your savings bank and ask for the current long-term rate. Enter this figure on Line 6, and multiply Line 5 by Line 6. Enter the result on Line 7. This is the amount you are losing this year by not having the use of your cash value.

Line 8 is your net annualized premium.

Add Line 4, Line 7, and Line 8. Enter the total on Line 9. This is how much it costs you to maintain your policy this year.

On Line 10, write the face amount of the policy, which you get from the first page. Enter the cash value again, on Line 11. Subtract Line 11 from Line 10 to get Line 12. This is your death benefit at risk. It is the amount the company is risking.

Insurance is priced in dollars per thousand. Write down the figure from Line 12 onto Line 13, and move the decimal three places to the left. (If Line 12 was 1,111, then line 13 will be 1.111.)

Divide Line 9 by Line 13 and enter the result on Line 14. This is what you are paying for your insurance, per one thousand dollars of death protection.

Whatever the cost per thousand, compare it with the figures given in the comparison table in Chapter 10. If you can buy insurance for less than you are paying now, I would recommend that you cancel this policy, invest the cash value, and purchase new insurance. Your other options are the same as those I outlined for Joe earlier in this chapter. If you can invest the cash value at a significantly higher rate of interest than the interest the company charges, an option is to borrow, invest, and pay the premiums with the difference. This is the most attractive choice if you are uninsurable and stuck with the policy you've got. Other options include cashing in the policy and investing the cash value, and taking paid-up or extended term insurance.

Chapter 13

The Edwards Case

This is the story of the case that changed my life. If this book helps to improve your insurance program and saves you money, this case may change your life too—and the lives of your survivors.

One day I met a nice young fellow we'll call Jack Edwards. He said he was an accountant. When he mentioned the family yacht, I became very interested.

The city directory told me all I needed to know. He worked for his father, Harry Edwards. And Harry Edwards was the head of a multimillion-dollar close corporation, which operated several successful automobile dealerships.

I had found gold. Now I had to mine it.

Over a period of weeks I had further chats with Jack. We had lunch. He asked me what I thought about term insurance. Let me tell you, I weighed my words carefully.

"Under certain conditions," I said, "term insurance can serve a very useful purpose in the insurance program."

I could see that he was impressed. Obviously other insurance salesmen had been pressuring the Edwards family to buy permanent insurance. Later Jack told me that I was the first insurance man he felt he could trust.

"Frankly," he said, "I just don't feel secure with my father's insurance agent. I don't think my father trusts him, either. But I feel like I can trust you."

I wrote his father a letter offering my services as an estate analyst. I told Jack I had written him and said I would appreciate it if he would say a word on my behalf. He did, and because of his intercession Mr. Edwards agreed to see me.

The corporation had an outside accountant in addition to Jack, and a tax lawyer. Mr. Edwards knew that working up an estate analysis is a big job. He asked, as people always do, what was in it for me.

I gave the answer that every estate analyst always gives.

"We don't know at this point whether my analysis will reveal any problems, Mr. Edwards," I said, "let alone whether insurance will be the answer. If the analysis does indicate the need for insurance, I hope that you will consider my further services. If there is no indication that insurance is called for, then I'd appreciate your comments on my work if I should give your name as a reference. That would mean a great deal to me, and would make any effort on my part worthwhile."

That, of course, like my earlier remark to his son about term insurance, was absolute hogwash.

But it never fails. He honestly believed he was so important that his recommendations would be compensation for hours of my work. After further luncheons and discussions, Mr. Edwards agreed to let me do his estate analysis, just as I knew he would.

Mr. Edwards' accountant gave me some figures to work with, and I began the analysis. After several hours I realized something was wrong. I called the accountant and made another appointment with him. By the time we met I had ascertained that he had merely sloughed off some figures on me. I was finally able to convince him that I had to have accurate and detailed figures, and this time he provided them. I had to do the whole thing all over again.

I am a painstaking, fastidious financial analyst, and my report impressed Mr. Edwards, his son, and his accountant. It showed that if Mr. Edwards died, he would need $352,000 additional insurance in order to pay federal and state taxes and leave the estate unencumbered to his heirs.

My recommendation was for Mr. Edwards to create an irrevocable trust for the purpose of owning a policy for that amount and, on Mr. Edwards' death, of paying the inheritance taxes. The corporation would pay the premiums.

Jack and I continued to have lunch together every few days while Mr. Edwards was making up his mind. Jack kept bringing up term insurance. "I've never really seen an analysis on the difference between permanent and term," he said one day.

I never had, either. If a thorough analysis had ever been done by anyone, anywhere, up to that time, I had never seen it, and I was very well read in the technical journals and publications of my profession. Everything I had read on the subject was written by and for insurance men, and dismissed term insurance without going into details.

The idea of doing such an analysis myself intrigued me more and more. Then I would know, once and for all, based on my own computations, the answer to the burning question, term versus perm. It was becoming obvious that the Edwardses wanted to see an analysis before they bought the $352,000 worth of life insurance I recommended and were willing to make some compensation for my time. I love to work with figures, and I thought, well, here's a good excuse to take a week and have some fun and prove to my client and to myself that permanent insurance is the more financially sound method of providing death benefits. So before they demanded it, I proposed to Mr. Edwards that I would prepare a detailed comparison of the various insurance options open to him. He said that he would be glad to look at my presentation. What more could I ask? I went to work.

The first step was to secure ledger statements from the company. Amount of insurance: $352,000. Mr. Edwards' age: 55. I asked for computer printouts on three insurance plans: annual renewable term, participating whole life, and non-participating whole life. I had no intention of laying three blurry printouts of a lot of numbers before Mr. Edwards, Jack, and their accountant. Therefore I will not reproduce them here, either. I will show the appropriate figures in their proper places.

A figure that never came up was my commission. On the one-year term, initial annual premium $4,170, I would receive 42 percent, or $1,751. For the non-par whole life, annual premium $11,995, I would receive 102 percent commission, or $12,235. For the participating whole life, premium $17,151, I would receive 85 percent, or $14,578. Although my highest commission would come from the participating whole life, I decided to make my play for the non-par. The people I was dealing with would know that I would receive some form of compensation. I figured that not recommending the highest premium would make my presentation more convincing. Of course, the lower commission rate was a factor.

My presentation would go far beyond the ledger statements. It would show the comparative real costs of the three different plans in relationship to the real benefits. Sounds simple until you start doing it. I went through a lot of work sheets, experimental tables, and many hours before coming up with a procedure for making a comparison. It was composed of the following tables:

1.   Net Premium Comparison
1-A. Gross Premium Comparison
2.   Net Cost Comparison
2-A. Total Death Benefit

I will explain them in detail when I present them. My major mission was to show Mr. Edwards which plan would be most advisable to buy. With all tables except Table 1, the time value of money had to be considered. For Tables 2 and 2-A this involved taking the difference in the premiums of the three plans and investing it in a side fund at compound interest. To clarify that very simply, I subtracted each of the cheaper premiums from the most expensive, and set up imaginary accounts with the resulting amounts. For Table 1-A this involved compounding the cumulative premiums. I chose an interest rate of 7 percent, and went to work.

I don't remember how many days and nights I put in on the first set, but I remember well how I felt when I finished.

I was sick all over. My figures showed conclusively that term insurance was by far the best deal.

I saw myself wasting all that time, all that work, and losing all that money. *What could I do?* I thought of all kinds of things.

A less expensive whole life policy? This was the company's best.

A more expensive term policy? The one I was using was already unusually high.

A lower rate of interest? Aha! I threw the work sheets using 7 percent in the trash basket and worked it all out again at 5 percent. This time the figures made the whole life look better than term on the Net Cost Comparison table.

But even the combination of low interest and high term premium couldn't save the Gross Premium Comparison and Total Death Benefit tables. Oh my God, I thought. What have I gotten myself into? All along I had had a terrible feeling that I should never have taken on this project, that I might find out something I did not want to know.

It never occurred to me to give up and sell the term insurance. I was in too deep to quit. I kept thinking, and over a period of days I worked out an approach. One thing I had going for me—I knew the value of a properly prepared presentation.

And so, when I determined what tables I would present, I typed them myself, on an IBM Selectric. Each table was neat, clean, and errorless. I made the copies myself, and they too were perfect. I placed each set in a dark blue vinyl cover with my letterhead on the front in gold. I handed one set each to Mr. Edwards, Jack, and the accountant, and provided another for the attorney, who did not attend. We sat around a table, our folders in front of us.

These are the exact figures. You are seeing just what they saw.

The presentation compares three plans. Reading from left to right, first you see three columns of figures dealing with a one-year-renewable term policy. The initial annual premium of this policy was $4,170 ($11.85 per thousand). This was a high-cost policy; the company has since reduced the premiums. As you read down the column you will see that the premiums increase each year to the sixteenth year, or age 70. At that age this policy was no longer renewable. The insured would have to take out instead a permanent policy, the premiums of which, as you can see in the sixteenth year, would be much higher.

The second plan was non-participating whole life. The annual premium, from the first year on, was $11,995.

The third plan was participating whole life. In this plan the company would pay dividends after the first year and the dividends would be used to reduce the premium. You see, therefore, that the first year's premium is $17,151, and this number decreases each year as the dividends are paid. The

TABLE 1
NET PREMIUM COMPARISON ON $352,000

Year	One-Year Term			Non-Par Whole Life			Par Whole Life		
	Annual Premium	Cumulative Premiums	Cash Value	Annual Premium	Cumulative Premiums	Cash Value	Annual Premium	Cumulative Premiums	Cash Value
1	$4,170	$4,170	None	$11,995	$11,995	None	$17,151	$17,151	$5,632
2	4,892	9,062	None	11,995	23,990	4,576	15,782	32,933	17,248
3	5,328	14,390	None	11,995	35,985	14,784	15,416	48,349	28,512
4	5,800	20,190	None	11,995	47,980	24,992	15,056	63,405	40,128
5	6,317	26,507	None	11,995	59,975	35,200	14,704	78,109	51,392
6	6,884	33,391	None	11,995	71,970	45,760	14,352	92,461	62,656
7	7,496	40,888	None	11,995	83,965	55,968	13,993	106,454	73,920
8	8,169	49,056	None	11,995	95,960	65,824	13,641	120,095	84,480
9	8,901	57,957	None	11,995	107,955	76,032	13,286	133,381	94,336
10	9,700	67,657	None	11,995	119,950	85,888	12,930	146,311	104,544
11	10,580	78,237	None	11,995	131,945	96,096	12,571	158,882	114,048
12	11,552	89,789	None	11,995	143,940	105,600	12,191	171,073	123,904
13	12,618	102,407	None	11,995	155,935	115,104	11,790	182,863	133,056
14	13,787	116,194	None	11,995	167,930	124,608	11,368	194,231	142,208
15	15,033	131,226	None	11,995	179,925	133,760	10,987	205,218	151,360
16	25,885	157,111	None	11,995	191,920	142,560	10,653	215,871	159,808
17	25,885	182,996	13,728	11,995	203,915	151,360	10,308	226,179	168,256
18	25,885	208,881	28,160	11,995	215,910	160,160	9,935	236,114	176,704
19	25,885	234,766	42,592	11,995	227,905	168,608	9,586	245,700	184,800
20	25,885	260,651	56,672	11,995	239,900	177,408	9,294	254,994	192,896

dividends are not guaranteed, of course; I used estimates provided by the company.

Each plan is divided into three columns:

ANNUAL PREMIUM	CUMULATIVE PREMIUMS	CASH VALUE

I explained this to the three men. Then I said, "Now, Mr. Edwards, I would like you to look at the One-Year Term, fifteenth year, for example. You will see that the cumulative premiums—that is, all of the premiums that you will have paid through that year—amount to $131,226 minus the cash value. The cash value is, as you see, none. Therefore, at the end of the fifteenth year, this policy has cost you a total of $131,226 in premiums."

I paused as Mr. Edwards, Jack, and the accountant followed the figures on their copy. Mr. Edwards nodded, and I proceeded.

"Now go to the section marked Non-Par Whole Life. Follow it down to the fifteenth year. You see that the cumulative premiums amount to $179,925. But the cash value of this policy in the fifteenth year is $133,760. Now if we subtract $133,760 from $179,925"—four pencils were busy—"we get $46,165. Let me put that another way. If you quit the plan at the end of the fifteenth year, you would have paid in $179,925. The insurance company would return to you $133,760, which means that you would have paid a total of $46,165 for fifteen years of being insured with a death benefit of $352,000."

They all saw that, too.

"Now let us go to the last three columns, Participating Whole Life. As you can see, at the end of the fifteenth year, you would have paid in $205,218 in cumulative premiums, including the refunded dividends, and your cash value would be $151,360. Thus you would pay premiums of $53,858 to have this participating whole life policy for fifteen years."

We discussed this table for some time, taking other years and comparing them, but there was no argument. There couldn't be. Simple arithmetic showed that every year, if he quit the insurance program completely, the non-par whole life program would have cost him less in premiums.

"I know you are interested in the concept of term insurance," I said, "and as your advisor I want to do everything I can to help you explore it thoroughly. But we are dealing here with a permanent need, and these figures demonstrate that the answer to that permanent need is permanent life insurance."

This is where most insurance salesmen would close their presentation—and close the sale. It still amazes me that sophisticated businessmen buy large amounts of insurance on this type of presentation. In this case, however, I knew that Jack Edwards, a CPA, was going to study this carefully. As I needed his endorsement to sell his father, I had to go deeper.

We relaxed a few moments, and then I suggested we look at Table 2.

TABLE 2
NET COST COMPARISON
$17,151 ANNUAL PREMIUM

Policy Surrendered End of Year	One-Year Term + Fund*	Non-Par Whole Life + Fund*	Par Whole Life + Fund*
5	$16,710	$20,640	$25,811
10	31,233	17,528	35,884
15	51,860	6,683	35,308
20	131,539	(13,401)	18,468

*Assumes 5% net earnings compounded annually

"What we are doing here," I said, "is comparing the real cost to you of these three policies, taking into consideration the premise that you would invest the difference in the premiums of the three policies in a special fund."

(Sound familiar? This is the time value of money again.) I went on to explain it fully.

The figure $17,151, annual premium of Par Whole Life, was the highest initial annual premium of all three plans. Let us assume that Mr. Edwards was going to apply this amount to his insurance program every year.

The first column of figures, One-Year Term + Fund, is derived by subtracting each year the amount of the annual premium of the term policy from $17,151, and investing that amount at 5 percent, then for years 5, 10, etc., subtracting that total (fund) from total premiums paid. To arrive at the figure for the first year, for example, we go to Table 1, look under One-Year Term, and get the figure $4,170. Subtract that figure from $17,151. This gives us $12,981, the difference between what Mr. Edwards would pay for term and participating whole life insurance. Invested at 5 percent, the interest is $649. Added to $12,981, the total fund for year one is $13,630. We now subtract that amount from $17,151 (total premiums paid) to get $3,521, the net cost of the term for one year. I did not show this detailed work, of course, just the five-year accumulations.

We followed the same procedure for the second column, non-par whole life plus the difference invested at 5 percent interest. But notice, as directed in the first column, that this is based on Mr. Edwards' *surrendering* the policy and drawing the cash value listed on Table 1 as well.

The third column, for participating whole life, is a bit more complicated. For this we have to take the premium paid in each year, subtract the dividend from it, and subtract that result from the master figure of $17,151 to get the side fund. This column also takes into account the cash surrender value, of course.

This table showed Mr. Edwards what a really honest fellow Walt Kenton was. He could really count on me, because you will see that up to the fifth year, term insurance is the best buy. But long before the tenth year, the non-par whole life has improved significantly. In twenty years, the chart shows, Mr. Edwards would actually get back $13,401 more than he paid in.

The two charts together proved conclusively the advantages of non-participating whole life insurance. I could tell that all three men were impressed. Mr. Edwards asked if they could keep the presentations and think it over, and of course I agreed.

While waiting to hear from Mr. Edwards, you may be interested in looking at the tables I did not present, as well as taking a second look at those I did.

Let's go back to Table 1, Net Premium Comparison. This told Mr. Edwards how much he would pay (cumulative premiums less cash value) for each insurance plan, year by year. Right?

Wrong. The very title explains why: *Net* Premium Comparison.

It insinuates that Mr. Edwards has the use of the cash value to offset premiums, which he does not. Also, to keep the insurance in force, he must pay the full premium *and* forfeit the use of that premium. Premiums paid would be more accurately represented by the column Cumulative Premiums only if Mr. Edwards kept his money in a mattress. Since he doesn't, we must again consider the time value of money, the amount Mr. Edwards would have if he had invested his money at compound interest, instead of purchasing the insurance. We have discussed this before, in the *net cost method*. But let me refresh your memory.

Say you give me $1,000 every year for twenty years. I give you back $20,000. Are we even?

Of course we aren't. I will have invested that money and made more. You will not have invested it and lost more. Even at the low rate of 5 percent, which I am stuck with in this comparison, I will have $33,500. Thus when I give you back your $20,000, and you thank me sweetly, I will have the $13,500 you could have had but do not. At 10 percent, a more reasonable rate, I will have $43,000 left after I give you back your $20,000.

So you understand that for me to simply add up the premiums, subtract the cash value, and call the total premiums paid was ridiculous.

But that's exactly what I did and nobody contradicted me.

Then what would the total cumulative premiums amount to, year by year, for each policy? This would be shown in a *gross* premium comparison, which would include compound interest.

Remember, I had worked out these figures at 7 percent—and thrown them in the wastebasket as if they were crawling with bugs. I had also worked out the gross premium comparison at 5 percent. I got rid of those figures, too. Why? I will show you. I sure as hell did not show Harry Edwards.

Because I threw all my figures away, I have had to redo them completely for this book. These figures do not include the cash value of the permanent policies. This table shows only the amount of premiums paid at the time of death.

So here is the 5 percent table I did not show Harry Edwards.

You see that the first figure, first line, is $4,379. The premium for one-year term, you will recall, is $4,170. We are assuming that if Mr. Edwards invested that money, instead

TABLE 1-A
GROSS PREMIUM COMPARISON ON $352,000
Cost for insurance upon death, premiums compounded at 5%

Year	One-Year Term	Whole Life, Non-Par	Whole Life, Par
1	$4,379	$12,595	$18,009
2	9,735	25,819	35,480
3	15,816	39,705	53,441
4	22,697	54,285	71,922
5	30,465	69,594	90,957
10	83,529	158,415	195,428
15	174,023	271,777	318,001
20	372,284	416,457	463,813

of buying insurance with it, he would have received net interest of 5 percent. (That's a laugh. If he'd been satisfied with 5 percent, he'd never have made a million bucks and needed estate insurance in the first place.) Five percent of $4,170 is $208.50. Add that to $4,170, round it off, and the result is $4,379. To get line number two in the same column, we take that figure, $4,379, and add the second year's premium, $4,892, which gives us $9,271. Five percent interest is $464; the total is $9,735. I followed this procedure for each one of the three columns, using the annual premiums from Table 1.

At the time, incidentally, calculators were just coming into common usage. Today I would punch 1.05 and the memory key and save two steps. But then I did the computations as I described, at a cost of many hours.

Now let's look at line five, $30,465. If Mr. Edwards had bought term insurance and died at the end of the fifth year, this is the actual amount it would have cost him. Put another way, this is the amount he would have if instead of buying insurance he had invested those premiums at a net rate of 5 percent.

Reading across the page, we see that the equivalent figure for Whole Life, Non-Par, is $69,594, and the figure for Whole Life, Par, is $90,957. Thus, the cost of term insurance was much less than the other two plans that year. Indeed, if you follow all three columns down the page, you will see that term insurance costs less every year.

And that is why Harry Edwards never saw this chart.

Table 2, you recall, took into consideration what Mr. Edwards would receive if he cashed in his policy. Table 2-A will show what his estate would receive upon his death. Again I used the largest premium, $17,151, and set up theoretical side funds with the difference. On Mr. Edwards' death, his estate would receive the face amount of the policy, $352,000, plus the side fund.

To demonstrate, subtract the first year's term premium,

TABLE 2-A
TOTAL DEATH BENEFIT
$17,151 ANNUAL PREMIUM
Side fund compounded at 5%

Year	One-Year, Term	Whole Life, Non-Par	Whole Life, Par
1	$365,630	$357,414	$352,000
2	379,184	363,098	353,437
3	392,957	369,067	355,331
4	406,923	375,334	357,697
5	421,045	381,915	360,552
10	492,277	420,094	383,082
15	557,406	468,822	422,597
20	563,482	531,012	483,656

$4,170, from the par premium, $17,151, and you get $12,981. Multiply by 1.05 and you get $13,630; add that to $352,000, and there is the first figure in the first column: $365,630. So you see that at the fifth year, term plus side fund is $421,045, non-par whole life plus side fund is $381,915, and par whole life is $360,552. The first column is larger every year. Even in the fifteenth to twentieth years, with an expensive whole life premium replacing term, the term death benefit plus side fund is greater.

Table 1-A shows Mr. Edwards would pay less for the term policy. Table 2-A shows it would pay his heirs more on his death. These are the important tables, not the ones I showed him.

Throughout this entire chapter, just as was actually the case in my presentation and subsequent deliberations, we have sailed right over the glaring flaw in this argument for whole life insurance. It sticks out like a naked light bulb. I even called attention to it. Yet Mr. Edwards, his son, his accountant, and his lawyer did not see it. How about you?

Let me repeat a couple of clues.

Remember, I told Mr. Edwards that as this was a *permanent* need, the answer was *permanent* insurance. "Permanent need" meant he needed it permanently, all his life.

He was buying this insurance for the sole purpose of paying his taxes when he dies, so that his survivors will inherit his estate in its entirety. Under terms of the law, he was going to put this insurance into an irrevocable trust; even if he goes broke and loses his shirt, he can't touch this insurance.

And so I based my entire sales presentation on showing him how, by using the cash value in his permanent insurance, the cumulative cost of non-par whole life is less than the other two plans.

But Mr. Edwards wasn't buying this insurance to cash it in. He was buying it for the express purpose of utilizing its *death benefits.*

Yet he and two certified public accountants sat there with my presentation, each neat and errorless copy inserted in handsome dark blue vinyl covers with my name stamped on them in gold, and never realized that the cash value I was selling him at 102 percent commission was of no value whatsoever.

A week after the meeting, during which time they had all gone over my charts again, Jack called.

"I can't tell you how much I appreciate this, Walt," he said. "This is the first time that I feel I really understand insurance. At last I can feel with assurance that permanent insurance is the best plan. My father agrees completely, and I am certain he is going to authorize you to write the policy."

Victory! I had come out ahead in a most difficult case, one man against four. To the thrill of winning add a commission of $12,235.

It didn't stop there. This was why the top executives had signed me up: to sell high-cost permanent insurance. My performance made them look good and would please the board of directors and the stockholders.

It justified the years of training invested in me by the insurance industry; this was what I had been taught to do. My fellow members of the American Society of CLU, of the Million Dollar Round Table, could all be proud of me—one of their boys had done it again. I could hear the cheers of the life insurance salesmen, 300,000 strong!

This was one hell of a time, therefore, for me to start having blinding headaches. I'd be riding along in my Cadillac, successful and prosperous, when *blam!*—something would hit me between the eyes.

And insomnia. I'd never had insomnia in my life. Why in the world, lying in a luxurious bed in the dream home Cathy and I had planned and built and just moved into, did I awaken, covered with sweat, at four o'clock in the morning and not be able to go back to sleep?

I was tired all the time, and cross and impatient. I wondered what was wrong with me. Was I getting tired of selling insurance? But what else could I do? I was trained for nothing else. I had developed a taste for fine food and wines and digital recordings. I continued prospecting for clients, taking them to lunch, keeping up my contacts. I went from aspirin to Excedrin.

One night Cathy and I visited an old friend, a doctor. Towards the end of the evening he observed that I had changed. I asked how.

"Oh, in little ways," he said. "I don't know that you are happy selling life insurance anymore."

I thought about what he said driving home that night. How could I not sell life insurance? I started talking about it to Cathy, and suddenly I found myself explaining to her for the first time the complete details of the Edwards case.

That led to another case, and another. I must have told her half a dozen cases, in all of which I had sold expensive, permanent insurance policies. And now I knew, thanks to the work I had done for Mr. Edwards, that those high-cost policies were not in the best interest of my clients, but in the best interest of the insurance industry.

I poured the whole thing out, and I think I was as surprised as Cathy to realize what I really thought about my life, my career, and me.

"I'd like to just chuck it out and write a book telling people the truth about life insurance," I said.

Here is a woman riding along in a Cadillac on the way to a big new house with a big new mortgage, hearing her husband say he is thinking of quitting the only thing he can do for a living. All she said was, "I think that's a million-dollar idea."

I didn't know how to write a book. I don't even read books. I only knew one person in the whole wide world who does know anything about books—he had a locker next to mine at the sports club. He took some notes, and a couple of weeks later he called and said that a big publisher wanted my book.

Shortly after that I called on a prospect for estate analysis. I was asked instead if I would be interested in the position of Director of Estate Planning for a small women's college.

I can't believe it. Now I am doing important work in something I can honestly believe in, and Cathy is going to college to get the degree she always wanted. We live in a pleasant little town near the college. For the first time in our lives we have real friends—people we like to be with, instead of people we are trying to cultivate and sell things to. I am bringing out a book that is going to benefit you and everybody else who reads it and needs insurance.

And the Edwards case? After we went through all that hassle, Mrs. Edwards, whom I never even saw, vetoed the whole deal and I never made a nickel.

Incidentally, I've often wondered what Table 2 would look like with a more competitive term policy and a realistic rate of interest. The company now does offer such a policy, renewable to age seventy-five. I have redone Table 2 using the figures from the new policy, and an interest rate of 10 percent. It speaks for itself as Table 3.

TABLE 3
NET COST COMPARISON AT 10 PERCENT
$17,151 ANNUAL PREMIUM

Year	One-Year Term + Fund	Non-Par Whole Life + Fund	Par Whole Life + Fund
5	$212	$15,929	$24,823
10	(34,303)	(4,769)	28,478
15	(110,928)	(56,696)	8,369
20	(229,023)	(159,229)	(54,844)

Chapter 14

Mr. Perm and Mr. Term

Convincing as the figures in the Edwards case may have been, they were for a large amount of insurance and applied to a man aged fifty-five. What about a more typical policy? Would the superiority of term insurance hold up?

I had never seen any figures on this that I could trust. The only way to provide meaningful data was to do the whole thing myself. So I did.

I wish I could show all my computations to those of you who, like me, get a kick out of working with figures. This was one of the most rewarding experiences of my life, and I'd like to share every decimal point.

But not everybody enjoys checking out work sheets, so I will include only enough figures to prove the accuracy of the computations. I did them twice, using a hand-held calculator, then I ran them through an OSI Challenger III computer. The figures are correct. I have the printouts on file for anybody who questions them. And they will prove some points about life insurance that you're not going to find anywhere else in the world.

I got the basic figures from the ledger statement I discussed in Chapter 6. It was printed to my order for a twenty-five-year-old prospect. The plan is permanent insurance, non-participating, face amount $100,000, premium $885. It is an actual policy from a well-known, reliable, competitive company, Integon Life Insurance Corporation. If it had been listed by Consumers Union in its report on life insurance, in February and March 1980, it would have been No. 6 on the rating. This is a good buy in permanent life insurance. I have sold this policy many times.

Let us say that at this moment, at a Jaycee meeting, at church, or in the locker room, a sharp life insurance salesman such as I used to be meets a young man who appears to be inordinately happy. The salesman has no difficulty learning that the young man is happily married with one child and plans for more, and has just gotten a big fat raise. So the salesman uses all his wiles, sells him this policy, and pockets $902.70 commission—102 percent of $885. He will continue to receive a commission, though at much smaller percentages, as long as the premiums are paid. This is permanent insurance, of course, and from now on we are going to refer to the insured as Mr. Perm.

The next day the salesman meets another prospect of the same age, same needs, and same ability to pay. This fellow, however, has read a new book by Walt Kenton, and he's not about to throw his hard-earned money away on permanent insurance.

"I'll spend $885 a year to protect my family," he says, "but I'll do it my way. I will buy a $100,000 term policy and invest the difference."

The salesman uses every argument he has been taught, and a few more he dreamed up himself, but the prospect is adamant. The salesman finally realizes he can sell either term insurance or nothing at all. The salesman gives up and writes a $100,000 term policy. So we shall call this purchaser Mr. Term.

Now for the term insurance policy. To keep this illustration honest, I have gone to the same company. This policy, too, is non-participating. The annual premium for the first year is $203 and increases each year. As we have seen on the comparison costs table in Chapter 9, there are term policies that sell for less. But I could also have found policies with premiums a great deal higher. This policy would rank No. 10 on the list of comparable policies on the CU list. It is a good buy, and generally available. The salesman? He gets 42 percent, or $85.26, and will continue to receive a commission, at much smaller percentages, on renewals.

Let me summarize this. I want you to be certain that I am not pulling any clever tricks. I am using two popular, available policies, each with a good price rating in its own category, each non-participating.

We are now ready to begin. Take a quick look at the table marked "Mr. Perm versus Mr. Term, Non-Par."

Column 1 is the age of the insured, Column 2, the age of the policy. Column 3 is the premium, $885, for the $100,000 permanent life insurance policy. Note that it stays the same all the way down.

Column 4 is the premium for the term policy. Note that it increases each year. At age 94, Mr. Term will pay $38,847 for this policy.

The difference between $885 and the premium for term is shown in Column 5. It's what you do with that difference that counts. Mr. Term is going to invest it.

Now I am not an investment advisor, so I will not attempt to suggest a sophisticated investment program. One of the least complicated and most conservative investment plans is an account in a federally insured savings and loan association. At this writing, anyone with a minimum of $100 can deposit it in a savings bank for a period of two and a half

MR. PERM VERSUS MR. TERM, NON-PAR

1 AGE	2 YEAR	3 P	4 T	5 P−T	6 SF	7 SF	8 CV	9 DB(P)	10 DB(T)
25	1	$885	$203	$682	$750	$750	$0	$100,000	$100,750
26	2	885	204	681	1,574	1,574	0	100,000	101,574
27	3	885	205	680	2,480	2,480	200	100,000	102,480
28	4	885	206	679	3,475	3,475	1,200	100,000	103,475
29	5	885	208	677	4,567	4,567	2,200	100,000	104,567
30	6	885	210	675	5,766	5,766	3,300	100,000	105,766
35	11	885	242	643	13,722	13,722	9,300	100,000	113,722
40	16	885	332	553	26,111	26,111	16,100	100,000	126,111
45	21	885	485	400	45,229	45,229	24,100	100,000	145,229
50	26	885	723	162	74,695	74,695	32,700	100,000	174,695
55	31	885	1,112	−227	120,028	120,437	41,700	100,000	220,028
60	36	885	1,748	−863	189,558	193,965	50,000	100,000	289,558
65	41	885	2,768	−1,883	296,003	312,383	58,200	100,000	396,003
70	46	885	4,721	−3,836	457,344	503,096	65,900	100,000	557,344
75	51	885	8,057	−7,172	699,045	810,242	72,800	100,000	799,045
80	56	885	13,015	−12,130	1,059,862	1,304,903	78,900	100,000	1,159,862
85	61	885	19,634	−18,749	1,601,418	2,101,559	84,000	100,000	1,701,418
90	66	885	27,951	−27,066	2,423,961	3,384,583	88,600	100,000	2,523,961
94	70	885	38,847	−37,962	3,379,760	4,955,368	92,800	100,000	3,479,760

EXPLANATION OF COLUMNS

1. Age of insured
2. Policy year
3. Premium for permanent (P) policy
4. Premium for term (T) policy
5. Permanent premium less term premium
6. Side fund: difference invested at 10 percent
7. As explained more fully in the text, at age 54 the fund reaches $100,000, the amount of insurance desired. Mr. Term then stops paying premiums
8. Cash value of permanent policy
9. Death benefit, permanent policy
10. Death benefit, term plus side fund

years and receive an effective annual yield of 18.27 percent interest.

For this exercise I am using a more conservative figure, 10 percent. This figure bypasses the sticky question of taxes; at this writing, municipal bond funds are advertising a tax-free income of 10.73 percent.

Column 6 is the side fund that results when the difference (Column 5) is invested at 10 percent. You see on line 1 that the difference the first year is $682. That is what Mr. Term has to invest. Ten percent is $68.20. $682 plus $68.20 equals $750 (we round off all figures). Or punch $682 times 1.10 on your calculator and round it off to $750. Mr. Term has that amount in his side fund at the end of the first year.

The second line down in Column 6 represents the previous year's figure plus the difference between $885 and the current premium, invested at 10 percent: $750 + $681 × 1.10 = $1,574.

Now to Column 7. It presents an interesting option. Mr. Term's original purpose was to leave $100,000 when he dies. At age 54 his side fund reaches that figure: $109,343 to be exact. He would be wise to stop paying premiums and just let his side fund continue to grow.

Column 8 shows the much-vaunted cash value in the permanent insurance policy. Compare it to the side fund and shed a tear for all those millions with permanent insurance.

Columns 9 and 10 compare death benefits. This, let me remind you, is the whole point of life insurance: money if you die. According to the mortality tables on which both policies are based, 18,481 of ten million young men will die at age twenty-five. This was a conservative figure to begin with, and the actual mortality rate has been decreasing. But still some twenty-five-year-olds will die.

If one of them is Mr. Perm, his heirs will receive the face value of his policy, $100,000, and that's all, from now to eternity. Cash value? It disappears. The death benefit, Column 9, never increases.

Mr. Term's heirs, on the other hand, also receive the face value of the policy, $100,000, *plus* the side fund, as shown in Column 10.

Now that we are familiar with the horizontal definitions, let's take a look at the impact. Pick an age, your age, my age, any age, look at the closest five-year increment, and see what would have happened if you had begun this program at age twenty-five.

I am forty. Let's look at age forty on the table. If I had bought permanent insurance at the age of twenty-five, it would have a cash value of $16,100. My survivors would get $100,000.

But if I had bought term insurance and invested the difference, I'd have $26,111 in my side fund. *My survivors would get that too,* for a total of $126,111!

As long as they live, Mr. Term always has more in his side fund than Mr. Perm has in his cash value. Mr. Term always has use of that side fund without jeopardizing the face amount of his insurance.

But Mr. Perm must pay 8 percent, or whatever the company requires, to get his cash value—and on top of that, his face amount is reduced.

The primary goal of both is to leave their heirs $100,000. As we have seen, Mr. Term can do that after age 54 out of his side fund. He can stop paying premiums, draw instead $10,934 a year (10 percent interest of $109,343), and still leave $100,000 plus to his survivors.

Poor Mr. Perm has to pay premiums until he's one hundred years old before he has $100,000 in paid-up insurance.

The farther we go down the columns, the more interesting the figures are. Now I know why ledger statements stop at sixty-five. I had a devil of a time getting these additional ages. Nobody had ever asked for such figures before. Now here they are, printed for the first time.

You can see why companies don't spread them around. Take a look at age 90, say. The mortality tables show that

468,174 of the original group of ten million men will still be living, and the number may include Mr. Perm and Mr. Term.

If he dies at 90, Column 9 shows us that Mr. Perm's family still gets $100,000. But Column 7 shows that heirs of Mr. Term get over *three million bucks.* At 94, it's almost five million. If I'm still around at that time, I am going to recommend strongly that Mr. Term withdraw some cash and take me out to dinner with a couple of bottles of Château Lafite-Rothschild, Vintage 2025.

Unlikely as these astronomical figures seem, they are nevertheless overwhelming proof of what happens when your money works for you instead of for the insurance company. Now you know why insurance companies keep after you to pay the premium on your permanent policy. They know the time value of money! Alive or dead, cash value or death benefit, the combination of term insurance and side fund is the superior investment.

The four tables following summarize my points. All demonstrate the tremendous impact of the time value of money. Table 1 shows the amount of death benefit paid to the heirs of Mr. Term and Mr. Perm, at specified years, and Table 2 shows how much the death benefit cost. Table 3 shows the amount each would have if he quit the program at specified years, and Table 4 shows how much it would have cost him.

In Table 1, look at the figures for age 65. The difference is $296,003. That is the amount the insurance company makes on the man with permanent insurance. Note that this table, like the others that follow, assumes that Mr. Term continues paying premiums, even after his side fund passes $100,000.

How much did it actually cost Mr. Perm and Mr. Term to provide a $100,000 death benefit? The only way to determine this is to figure out what they would have if they each invested $885 at 10 percent instead of paying out the money in premiums. The amounts are shown in Table 2. You will see that they are different.

TABLE 1
WHAT MY SURVIVORS WILL GET
WHEN I DIE

Age	Mr. Perm	Mr. Term
30	$100,000	$105,766
35	100,000	113,722
40	100,000	126,111
45	100,000	145,229
50	100,000	174,695
55	100,000	220,028
60	100,000	289,558
65	100,000	396,003
70	100,000	557,344
75	100,000	799,045
80	100,000	1,159,862
85	100,000	1,701,418
90	100,000	2,523,961

TABLE 2
WHAT DID THE INSURANCE
REALLY COST ME UPON MY DEATH?

Age	Mr. Perm	Mr. Term
30	$7,511	$1,745
35	18,040	4,318
40	34,997	8,886
45	62,306	17,077
50	106,288	31,593
55	177,122	57,094
60	291,200	101,642
65	474,923	178,920

But if both men are putting aside $885 a year, *why* are the figures different?

Because all of Mr. Perm's $885 went toward the cost of his insurance. A large share of Mr. Term's $885 (Column 5 in the Mr. Perm versus Mr. Term table) went into his side fund. And this side fund was returned to his survivors on his death, thus reducing the cost of his protection.

Note that Mr. Term's side fund stays with the family. Mr. Perm's cash value stays with the insurance company.

How old are *you* now? Note the difference between permanent and term at your closest age. What age do you plan to retire, 65? How much will you have paid for your insurance —$474,923 or $178,920? It's up to you.

Tables 1 and 2 are really all you need to know about buying life insurance. They show what your survivors get when you die, and they show what it cost you to leave them that money. What else matters?

But that is not the way life insurance salesmen sell life insurance. The industry has set up this thing called cash value and has trained its salesmen to feature it. I hope I have proved that you should not buy life insurance for cash value. It is a lousy investment. But because the life insurance industry stresses cash value, I have prepared these two tables showing the cash value Mr. Term and Mr. Perm would have if they stopped paying their premiums.

In Table 3 we see the cash value Mr. Perm has built up in his policy, compared with the side fund built up by Mr. Term. This proves that if you handle your savings yourself, you get back far more than if you let the company do it. Note how the compounding of your money increases your side fund with the years. If you have permanent insurance at age

TABLE 3
WHAT WILL I RECEIVE IF I QUIT?

Age	Mr. Perm	Mr. Term
30	$3,300	$5,766
35	9,300	13,722
40	16,100	26,111
45	24,100	45,229
50	32,700	74,695
55	41,700	120,028
60	50,000	189,558
65	58,200	296,003
70	65,900	457,344
75	72,800	699,045
80	78,900	1,059,862
85	84,000	1,601,418
90	88,600	2,423,961

65, you'll be able to cash in your policy for $58,200—and forfeit the rest of your insurance. With the same amount of money invested annually in term insurance and a side fund, you already have $296,003.

Table 2 showed how much the death benefit cost at specified years; Table 4 shows the cost of cashing in. We simply compound what each has spent, $885 per year, and subtract what they will get back. The figures for Mr. Term are identical to Table 2 because he receives his side fund whether he lives or dies. Mr. Perm gets his cash value only if he quits, so his cost to quit is lowered by those amounts. At any rate, if they quit, Mr. Perm gets back his cash value and Mr. Term gets back his side fund. You will see how each fares in Table 4. Who would you rather be?

TABLE 4
WHAT DID THE INSURANCE
REALLY COST ME WHEN I QUIT?

Age	Mr. Perm	Mr. Term
30	$4,211	$1,745
35	8,740	4,318
40	18,897	8,885
45	38,206	17,076
50	73,588	31,592
55	135,422	57,091
60	241,200	101,639
65	416,723	178,915

All of the tables so far have been based on non-participating policies. That is, Mr. Perm and Mr. Term paid a lower initial premium and received no dividends. But what would happen if they bought participating policies, which pay dividends?

Just about any person of reasonable intelligence can figure that the result would be the same—Mr. Term would come out ahead. That's right, he does. And I would like to leave it at that, except that the mutual companies would say I am fudging.

So, although I do not recommend the purchase of participating life insurance, and I knew it was going to be difficult to obtain figures to work with, I proceeded to work the whole thing out again with participating policies. I don't want to bore you with all these tables. However, if you are like me and you really like this sort of thing or if you doubt my figures and want to check them, you'll find the participating tables in the appendix.

Par or non-par, what these tables are saying is this: *Do not buy permanent, or cash value, life insurance.*

If you want to invest for the future, put your money in a plan that provides a higher yield.

If you want to provide money for those dependent on you if you should die tomorrow, buy term insurance.

If you want *both*—investment and death protection—buy term insurance and put the difference, or whatever amount you choose, in some form of secure investment.

Chapter 15

How Much Insurance Do You Need?

You now know that non-par term insurance is the best buy, but you're going to have trouble getting a salesman to sell it to you. He wants to sell you more expensive insurance because the premium is higher and his commission is higher. If you have only so much money to spend, he will push for a small amount of permanent insurance because he gets a larger commission for it than for a large amount of term insurance. Adequate protection for your family? Not at the expense of his!

When you have to deal with an insurance salesman, it will help you to know how much protection you need. You may need much more or much less than he says. And let me repeat, the "you" I'm talking to includes the working woman, in or out of the home. The more knowledgeable *you* are, the better coverage you will have at lower cost.

How, then, do you estimate fairly and accurately the amount of insurance you should have?

In this chapter I am going to show you. There are three different procedures, including a simple method for those who have not yet acquired a valuable estate and a complicated schedule for those who have. Even so, you may still want to complete the long forms. They give you a more accurate picture of your current net worth, and help you determine how much insurance you need to provide the same standard of living for your survivors if you should die.

The simplest method is the "six-times-salary" formula of the Teachers' Insurance and Annuity Association. It is short, sweet, and effective. If your income is between $10,000 and $25,000 a year and you have no additional financial complications, the following table will save you a lot of time. Buy the amount of protection it says. But keep this book and check back from year to year as your income and your estate increase.

1. Enter present annual salary $_____
2. Multiply by six   × 6
3. Minimum Family Protection goal $_____
4. Enter coverage you now have:
    (a) Personal policies $_____
    (b) Group insurance   _____
    (c) Pension plan death
        benefits   _____
5. Subtract total of (a) (b) (c) $_____
6. Additional insurance needed (if any) $_____

The next table is more sophisticated. It was printed in the July 1976 edition of *Consumer Views,* published by Citibank of New York, which has given me permission to use it. Though it has not been updated since that time, it is still an excellent tool. If anything, it errs on the high side; that is, it advises you to buy more insurance rather than not enough. The chart is designed to bring the surviving family's income, including Social Security survivor benefits, up to 60 or 75

MULTIPLES OF SALARY CHART

Your Present Gross Earnings	Present Age of Spouse							
	25 Years*		35 Years*		45 Years*		55 Years†	
	75%	60%	75%	60%	75%	60%	75%	60%
$7,500	4.0	3.0	5.5	4.0	7.5	5.5	6.5	4.5
9,000	4.0	3.0	5.5	4.0	7.5	5.5	6.5	4.5
15,000	4.5	3.0	6.5	4.5	8.0	6.0	7.0	5.5
23,500	6.5	4.5	8.0	5.5	8.5	6.5	7.5	5.5
30,000	7.5	5.0	8.0	6.0	8.5	6.5	7.0	5.5
40,000	7.5	5.0	8.0	6.0	8.0	6.0	7.0	5.5
65,000	7.5	5.5	7.5	6.0	7.5	6.0	6.5	5.0

*Assuming federal income taxes for a family of four (two children). There are four exemptions and the standard—or 15% itemized—deductions. State and local taxes are disregarded.

†Assuming you have only two exemptions. (Any children are now grown.)

percent of the insured's gross pay at the time of his death.

To use the chart, determine your gross annual salary. Find the appropriate line in the left-hand column. Follow that line across to the age of your wife. You will see the figure 75 percent, which will provide your survivors approximately the same income they are receiving now, or 60 percent, the minimum income. Decide which you want to provide, and multiply your salary by the code figure under the percentage. Example: Suppose you earn $40,000 a year, and your wife is thirty-five. To provide the optimum amount of insurance coverage, multiply $40,000 by eight; you need $320,000 worth of life insurance. If the premiums are too high, multiply your salary by the lower figure: $240,000. Your survivors would still be provided for, though not as generously.

If your wife will have other sources of income, such as an appreciable amount of investments or savings, pension or retirement benefits, add them up and subtract the total from the overall amount of insurance. The remainder is the amount of insurance you should have.

Although I am impressed with the simplicity and accuracy of this chart, I recommend to readers with moderately high incomes and large estates that you plan for your survivors more precisely. This requires a more complicated formula. The system I have worked out, the Insurance Estimator, with its tables and schedules, is something like an income tax form. Tedious as it may be, I believe that if you are a conscientious person with a substantial income and estate, you will have a warm feeling of satisfaction after you determine just how much insurance you really need and then provide it.

First, I am going to show you how to estimate the value of your estate. This service may be of more importance to you than you think. I have shown many people, after making an analysis of their estates, that thanks to inflation they are worth a great deal more than they thought.

If you follow my directions carefully you will achieve your own do-it-yourself estate analysis. Though I've had to simplify the procedure, the end result will approach what a topflight tax attorney, certified public accountant, or estate analyst would do for you. The attorney or CPA would charge from $500 up. The estate planner would pressure you to buy permanent life insurance.

You get an analysis of your estate for the price of this book.

Over the next few pages you will see forms and tables. They won't bite you. I've made them as simple as I possibly can and still be effective.

The first form, Insurance Estimator, is what you are going to wind up with. Glance at it now and you will understand all the other forms better. They will furnish the figures for the Insurance Estimator. Then skip over the forms to the text, and I'll tell you how to fill them out.

INSURANCE ESTIMATOR

Cash Needs

1. $_____ Final expenses
2. _____ Debts (adjust Schedule B Line 4?)
3. _____ Estate settlement—from Schedule A
4. _____ Mortgage (adjust Schedule B Line 4?)
5. _____ College
6. _____ Emergency fund
7. _____ Income—from Schedule B Line 14
8. _____ Total cash needs (Lines 1 through 7)

Cash Sources

9. $_____ Group life insurance
10. _____ Personal life insurance
11. _____ Liquid assets
12. _____ Non-liquid assets (adjust Schedule B Line 4?)
13. _____ Total cash sources (Lines 9 through 12)

Summary

14. $_____ Total cash needs (Line 8)
15. $_____ Total cash sources (Line 13)
16. $_____ Total additional life insurance needed (Line 14 less Line 15)

SCHEDULE A: INSURANCE ESTIMATOR
Calculations for Estate Settlement

1. $\_\_\_\_\_$ Fair market value of everything you own*

2. _____ Debts

3. _____ Gross estate (Line 1 less Line 2)

4. _____ Administrative expenses (Line 3 × 4.3%)

5. _____ Adjusted gross estate (Line 3 less Line 4).
   If more than $600,000, I recommend that
   you consult a tax attorney for planning
   techniques to minimize taxes on your estate
   if not married, and if married, on the estate
   of your surviving spouse.

6. _____ Marital deduction. (Total amount you wish
   to leave to surviving spouse not to exceed
   amount on Line 5.) Enter charitable
   bequests here also.

7. _____ Taxable estate (Line 5 less Line 6). Refer to
   Schedule A-1 and enter appropriate figure
   from Column D onto Insurance Estimator,
   Line 3.

*Include the following:
1. One-half value of property owned jointly with spouse.
2. Face amount of life insurance on your life if you have right to
   change beneficiary.

SCHEDULE A-1: ESTATE SETTLEMENT

(A) Taxable Estate	(B) Federal Estate Tax* 1982	1983	1984	1985	1986	1987 & Beyond	(C) Admin. Expenses	(D) Total
$250,000	$8,000	$---	$---	$---	$---	$---	$	$
300,000	25,000	8,500	---	---	---	---	$	$
350,000	42,000	25,500	8,500	---	---	---	$	$
400,000	59,000	42,500	25,500	---	---	---	$	$
450,000	76,000	59,500	42,500	17,000	---	---	$	$
500,000	93,000	76,500	59,500	34,000	---	---	$	$
600,000	130,000	113,500	96,500	71,000	37,000	---	$	$
700,000	167,000	150,500	133,500	108,000	74,000	37,000	$	$
800,000	205,000	188,500	171,500	146,000	112,000	75,000	$	$
900,000	244,000	227,500	210,500	185,000	151,000	114,000	$	$
1,000,000	283,000	266,500	249,500	224,000	190,000	153,000	$	$
1,250,000	385,500	369,000	352,000	326,500	292,500	255,500	$	$
1,500,000	493,000	476,500	459,500	434,000	400,000	363,000	$	$
1,750,000	605,500	589,000	572,000	546,500	512,500	475,500	$	$
2,000,000	718,000	701,500	684,500	659,000	625,000	588,000	$	$
3,000,000	1,228,000	1,211,500	1,194,500	1,054,000	1,120,000	1,083,000	$	$

*Includes credit for state death tax

SCHEDULE B: INSURANCE ESTIMATOR
Calculations for Additional Income Needed

Income Needs

1. $_____ Annual net (bring home) income of proposed insured

2. _____ Personal expenses and surplus income

3. _____ Family income needed (Line 1 less Line 2)

4. _____ Adjustments

5. _____ Adjusted family income needed

6. _____ Number of years this income is to continue

7. _____ Total income needed (Line 5 × Line 6)

Income Sources

8. $_____ Social Security—Table 1

9. _____ Social Security—Table 2

10. _____ Other

11. _____ Total income sources (Lines 8 through 10)

Summary

12. $_____ Total income needed (Line 7)

13. _____ Total income sources (Line 11)

14. _____ Additional income needed (Line 12 less Line 13)

Transfer to Insurance Estimator Line 7.

TABLE 1
SOCIAL SECURITY SURVIVORSHIP ESTIMATES FOR CHILDREN UNDER AGE 18

YOUR AGE	A	B
Under 30	$2,064	$6,174
30	1,908	5,724
35	1,788	5,376
40	1,716	5,160
45	1,668	5,034
50	1,644	4,944
55–64	1,644	4,932

With a surviving parent

$_____ Youngest child—multiply figure in Column B by 2 then multiply by years remaining until youngest child is age 17.*

$_____ Second youngest child—multiply figure in Column A by years remaining until next-to-the-youngest child is age 18.

$_____ Total—transfer to Schedule B, Line 8.

Without a surviving parent

$_____ Youngest child—multiply figure in Column B by years remaining until youngest child is age 18.

$_____ Second youngest child—multiply figure in Column B by years remaining until next-to-the-youngest child is age 18.

$_____ Third youngest child—multiply figure in Column A by years remaining until third youngest child is age 18.

$_____ Total—transfer to Schedule B, Line 8.

*Under provisions of 1981 legislation, parents' benefit (one-half of Column B) stops when child is age 16, but child receives benefit to age 18. Using age 17 here produces accurate results.

TABLE 2
SOCIAL SECURITY SURVIVORSHIP ESTIMATE FOR WIDOW OR WIDOWER AT AGE 60

YOUR AGE	
Under 30	$5,880
30	5,460
35	5,124
40	4,920
45	4,800
50	4,716
55–64	4,704

$_____ Multiply figure above by number of years adjusted family income is to continue (Line 6 on Schedule B) beyond surviving spouse's age 60. Transfer to Schedule B, Line 9.

Note: Figures in Tables 1 and 2 conform to 1981 legislation and are approximate due to bracketing of ages. Assumes eligibility for maximum benefit. Benefits as of January 1, 1981. No allowance for future increases due to inflation (automatic). Benefits are lower for physicians born prior to 1940.

HOW TO FILL IN THE FORMS

Begin with Schedule A: Calculations for Estate Settlement. This form will provide an estimate of your estate as it exists today. All these calculations should be repeated periodically, or when there is a major change in your financial or domestic situation.

Line 1: Fair market value of everything you own. If you have recently figured your net worth for tax or other purposes, you already have this figure. If not, here's how to compute it.

Include one-half the fair market value of all property owned jointly with spouse, including your house. In a community property state, list the market value of your property acquired prior to marriage, and one-half the value of property acquired after marriage. List the value of your business holdings (what a willing buyer will pay a willing seller). List the face amount of every life insurance policy you own. (You own it if you have the right to change the beneficiary. Otherwise, the owner will be named in the policy.) Include your automobiles, art objects, oriental rugs, boats, planes, race horses, shop equipment, precious gems, rare books, coin collections, each evaluated halfway between what you could get for it and what you tell the IRS it's worth. Include stocks and bonds, certificates of deposit, savings accounts.

Don't fudge on Line 1. It's the first figure you work from to calculate your insurance needs.

Line 2: Total all your debts, whether you plan to pay them off before your death or not. Anything you owe personally or one-half of what you owe on jointly owned property is a debt.

Subtract Line 2 from Line 1. The result is Line 3, Gross Estate.

Line 4: Administrative Expenses include attorney's fees, state probate costs, and executive fees. They average about 4.3 percent of a person's gross estate. Multiply Line 3 by .043

and enter the result on Line 4. Subtract Line 4 from Line 3 to get Line 5. This is your Adjusted Gross Estate.

If married, enter on Line 6 the total amount you are leaving your spouse in your will or by joint ownership. Your spouse must actually receive the property or all the income from the property in order to get the deduction. Include in Line 6 any charitable bequests.

Subtract Line 6 from Line 5, and there's your Taxable Estate, Line 7. If you've left everything to your spouse and/ or to charities, this line will equal zero, and thanks to the 1981 tax act, you will pay no tax. Otherwise, continue.

Schedule A-1, Estate Settlement, shows your estate taxes. Pick your number in Column A, add B, Federal Estate Tax, plus Column C, taken from Line 4 in Schedule A. The result is Column D, the amount your heirs will pay. Again, because of the 1981 act, it may be zero.

If there is a tax due and you wish to take out insurance for this amount, call me. But you'd be smarter to tell your heirs that under provision of Section 6166 of the IRS Code they may qualify to take fifteen years to pay a large portion of the taxes and pay 4 percent interest only the first five years. If they want your money, 4 percent is a reasonable price to pay for it.

It's an irony of life that many people who have an estate to leave their heirs also have insurance to add to that estate. It's a tragedy that many people who do not have an estate have no insurance, or inadequate insurance, to provide for those dependent upon their income.

Now we will try to advise those of you who support other people with your earnings. *How much insurance do you need to replace your income for them if you die?* Let's figure it out. Go to Schedule B, Calculations for Additional Income Needed.

Before you start filling in Schedule B, let me explain it. It is *not* what insurance salesmen are taught to use. They would work with your gross income, for example, because it provides a higher figure to start from. Your wife and children don't see your full salary, however. Much of it is withheld for deductions that will end with your death. Your survivors get along without those deductions now, and should not expect to receive them if you die.

On Line 1, enter your Annual Net Income. Don't include taxes, Social Security, hospitalization, or pension payment withheld from your paycheck. Put down your take-home pay, what your family depends on your bringing home.

Line 2 is a rough calculation of how much of that income goes to expenses *just for you,* expenses your survivors won't have. Your food, including lunch and drinks, clothing, extra car, doctor bills, cost of spectator sports and recreation sports, contributions, gambling losses, money you're socking away for some personal indulgence. Include every expense that will no longer exist once you are dead.

Subtract Line 2 from Line 1, and you have Line 3: Family Income Needed—the amount of income your family currently depends on from you. This is what insurance is for, so that if you die your family will continue to have what they need and enjoy.

Line 4: Adjustments. This is to take care of any additional or reduced income needs your family may incur if you die. For example, your survivors may need to purchase hospitalization insurance to replace your group plan, so add the estimated annual premium. On the other hand, if your insurance is going to pay the mortgage (Insurance Estimator, Line 4), then the mortgage payments will no longer have to be made and you can reduce the annual income needs accordingly—but remember taxes and insurance. If your spouse intends to sell the house, you can subtract the total annual payment—but don't forget to add rent.

Add or subtract Line 4 to get Line 5, Adjusted Family Income Needed. This is the amount of money your family will have to have per year after you are no longer there to provide it.

But this will not go on forever. At some point your children are going to be grown up and buying their own insurance. This is one of the big reasons why I recommend the purchase of low-cost term insurance and the annual reassessment of the amount needed. How many millions of people go on routinely paying their premiums long after their survivors no longer need the insurance! As the years go by and the family situation changes, adjust your insurance to fit the current need.

Now, you must decide how long you want to provide the amount of income you have determined. Until your youngest child reaches a certain age? Until your wife becomes eligible for Social Security benefits? Multiply the Adjusted Family Income figure by the number of years you want to provide it, and you come up with our final figure: Line 7, Total Income Needed. This figure does not take into account depreciation for time value of money or appreciation for inflation, as they will cancel each other out.

These are your family's income needs. Now let's consider a major income source, Social Security. Computing future Social Security benefits can get extremely complicated, particularly with continuing changes in the law. Insurance companies issue booklets for salesmen to use as door-openers, but they are usually oversimplified and even then the salesmen don't understand them. Consumers Union, which tries to do an honest job, presents so many charts, figures, factors, and options that the procedure is bewildering. I have spent many, many hours on this, and I believe I have come up with the first comprehensible Social Security Benefits Estimator. I am assuming, of course, that you have consistently paid into the system the maximum tax, and that you are currently covered.

Begin with Table 1, Social Security Survivorship Estimates for Children Under Age 18. If you have no children under the age of eighteen, you get no Social Security benefit, and you put down a big fat zero for Line 8 in Schedule B.

If you do have children, proceed with the table. Note that it has three columns: Your Age, Column A, and Column B.

Under these columns is the section marked With A Surviving Parent. Use this if your wife—or husband—is alive. The first blank is marked *youngest child.* Match your age to the appropriate figure in Column B. (If you are thirty-one to thirty-five, the figure is $5,376.) Multiply that figure by two. (2 × $5,376 = $10,752.) Deduct your youngest child's age from 17 and multiply again. (If the child's age is 7, subtract 7 from 17 to get 10. Multiply $10,752 by 10 = $107,520.) Enter the number in the blank.

The next blank is marked *second youngest child.* Take the figure from the appropriate line in Column A, and multiply by the second youngest child's age deducted from 18. (If the child is 10, 18 − 10 = 8 × $1,788 = $14,304.) Add the two figures to get the total, and enter on Schedule B, Line 8.

If your wife—or husband—is dead, go down to the section marked Without a Surviving Parent. For the first blank, *youngest child,* find the appropriate figure in Column B and multiply by the child's age subtracted from 18. Repeat for the second youngest child, i.e., multiply the appropriate figure in Column B by the second youngest child's age deducted from 18. For the third youngest child, get the appropriate figure from Column A and multiply by the age of that child deducted from 18. Total the figures and enter the amount on Line 8, Schedule B.

Go to Table 2, Social Security Survivorship Estimate for Widow or Widower at Age 60.

After the youngest child reaches 16, benefits for the surviving parent stop. But benefits resume when the parent reaches age 60. Did the number of years you entered on Line 6 of Schedule B go beyond your spouse's age 60? If not, put a zero here. If they did, find the figure in the right-hand column closest to your age and multiply that figure by the number of years this income will continue beyond your spouse's age 60. Enter on Line 9 of Schedule B.

Lines 8 and 9 represent the income from Social Security. What other income will your survivors have? Pension? Rents? Dividends? Interest from other investments? Whatever will be coming in, annualize the amount and enter on Line 10. Total Lines 8, 9, and 10 to get 11.

Now let's summarize what we have done on Schedule B thus far. On Line 12, enter the figure from Line 7. On Line 13, enter the figure from Line 11. Subtract Line 13 from Line 12, and you get Line 14, Additional Income Needed.

And now we will go to the Insurance Estimator to determine how much total life insurance you need.

On Line 1, we will put Final Expenses. I hope that you have hospitalization and disability insurance to provide for the gruesome possibility of a lingering terminal illness. If you do not have such insurance, you should allocate an estimated amount of money for dying. I'm sorry, but death is not always swift. Burial expenses can also be costly. A modest service in most localities would begin around $2,000. A more elaborate ceremony will cost $5,000. It is possible to pay many times that: you can buy an $18,000 casket. (At that price, it's called a sarcophagus.) If you're buried from St. Patrick's, with a procession of long black limousines, your funeral can cost a fortune. Whatever it is you want, provide for it. It is unfair to your survivors to allocate $2,500 for your funeral without specifying that amount in your instructions. Your grief-stricken wife will let herself get talked into a cast bronze sarcophagus and a dozen limousines.

It is possible to leave your survivors no funeral expenses at all. That is what I have done. I have left my body to a medical school. I will no longer be needing it, and it is nice to know that not only will it not cost anything to put it away but it will also continue to be of use to mankind after I am gone.

Line 2. This is for your debts, adjusted according to your plans. Do you wish everything to be paid immediately? If you owe $20,000 on your sports car and you want your insurance to take care of that debt, then enter it here. Check with Schedule B, Line 4, to make sure you have not provided insurance to pay for it twice. The annualized payment for any debts being paid off should be subtracted from income needs on Schedule B, Line 2 or Line 4.

Line 3. If you used Schedule A, transfer the appropriate figure from Column D, Schedule A-1.

Line 4. If you provide for the payment of the mortgage here, adjust Schedule B, Line 4, by subtracting the annualized principal and interest payment.

Line 5. When I was an insurance salesman I would remind you that the tuition for one year at Harvard Medical School will probably be $25,000 by the time your three-year-old child is accepted. Perish the thought that any of your children would go to a free community college, to Notre Dame on a full athletic scholarship, or to no college at all. I know that it is difficult for you to decide now how much money you want to provide for your children's college education, but I never said that all these decisions would be easy. If you decide to include college tuition in your insurance plans, consult *Barron's Profiles of American Colleges* for costs and adjust for inflation.

Line 6. I have had clients look at me as though I had lost my mind when I proposed that they provide a savings account for their wives to handle emergencies. "I never had a savings account," some say. "Why should my wife?" Other men immediately write down sums of up to $50,000. Maybe a cushion of a few thousand dollars would be a nice thing for a widow to have. Who knows what sudden requirements might pop up.

For Line 7, get the figure from Schedule B, Line 14. Total Lines 1 through 7. Line 8 is the total cash needed.

Now for the sources of cash to take care of all your survivors' problems. For Line 9, fill in the amount of group life insurance you have. I have separated group insurance from other insurance for your convenience in future years, if for some reason, like leaving your present position, you have to cancel it.

Line 10 is the personal insurance you have now. Do not include double indemnity and policies that pay off only if your airplane hits a streetcar. You just simply cannot count on dying in a beneficial way.

Line 11. Enter here assets that can be readily converted to cash.

Line 12 is specifically for the real estate you and your wife have agreed that she will not want after your death. If she is going to move out of the big, expensive house into a cozy apartment, then enter here what you know, not what you hope, the house will sell for. Don't forget to subtract the annualized mortgage payment and then add the annualized rent in Schedule B, Line 4.

Line 13. All the money not previously accounted for.

And now comes the grand finale, the figure we've all been waiting for. On Line 14 enter the total cash needs, on Line 15 the total cash sources. Subtracting Line 15 from Line 14 gives us Line 16, which is the total additional life insurance you need.

Chapter 16

How to Buy It

Now you know how much insurance you need. How are you going to get a low-cost policy for that amount?

Well, some people may find insurance easy to buy. We've discussed several possibilities. Persons connected with educational institutions, you recall, can buy TIAA insurance by calling (800) 223-1200. Those in the military, active or reserve or retired, can get insurance easily at competitive prices from the USAA Life Insurance company, a stock company, by calling (800) 531-8000. Group insurance where you work, or through a fraternal organization, professional society, or credit card, is easy to purchase. It may be much more expensive than an individual policy, however, because the rates reflect the entire spectrum of your group. Mail order insurance may be easy to purchase, but the hard sell and the gimmicks of the mail order offers I've seen would turn me off even if they weren't extremely high.

People in Massachusetts can stop in at the corner savings

bank and get a limited amount of term insurance at a good price without hassle. (Savings bank insurance in Connecticut and New York is also easily obtainable, but in lesser amounts at higher prices.)

A recent development is buying insurance through stockbrokers. Some of them list insurance among their services in the yellow pages. Because insurance is only a sideline and the commission on even a term policy is high in comparison to rates on sales of securities, stockbrokers may not push as hard to sell high-cost insurance. Just request a low-cost policy and let them fill your order. Make sure, by comparing it with the prices quoted in Chapter 10, that it *is* low cost.

Further, they have no inhibitions about switching, and some national agencies, like A. G. Edwards and Sons, will run the necessary paper work through their computer as a matter of course. In exchange for this service they get their foot in your door to handle your investments.

If you go to an insurance agency, you must remember that no salesman wants to sell you term insurance. The commission is a double low—low percentage of a low premium—and the sale takes you out of the market.

On the other hand, if you call an agency and say, "I want to buy some life insurance," you have saved them the time and expense of finding you, selling you, and working up your needs. You're entitled to service.

The yellow pages in the telephone directory list both branch offices of major companies and general agencies. Do not call the branch office. They sell only one company's products. Call the general agency instead, preferably one with an ad listing several companies.

If you want to call an agent who's a friend or relative or neighbor or member of your church or club, okay. But do not expect him to agree immediately and happily to lose money by selling you low-cost insurance. You will have an argument.

Whoever you call, once you have the salesman on the line,

identify yourself and say: "I want to buy an annual renewable term policy with a face value of $——. I am —— years old. Please check your rate cards and call me back with your lowest rate."

The salesman will want first to set up an appointment to get his foot in your door.

"Well, I'm going to call a few other agencies, and if someone else's premium is lower, you'd just be wasting a trip. Look at your rate cards for annual renewable term, revertible if you have it, and call me back."

In a large metropolitan area there will be pages of agencies and you may have to call several before you get a price in line with those given in the comparison table in Chapter 10. Don't be discouraged. Many insurance companies today offer competitive rates. Sooner or later you will find an agency that represents a competitive company.

In a small community there will be fewer agencies, which perhaps handle only companies writing high-cost term policies. Don't fuss at them if their prices are out of line. It is entirely probable that they just aren't aware that other companies offer lower cost policies. There's no reason they should know, for you may be the first person to ask for a competitive price.

But do not let them tell you they cannot sell you a low-cost policy because they are not licensed with low-cost companies. They are wrong. An agency can sell almost any company's product on what is officially known as a *one-time basis*. Remind them of this, and suggest some companies they can call.

Your library will have the February 1980 issue of *Consumer Reports*. On pages 97, 98, and 99 it presents its list of forty lowest cost policies, non-participating. In addition, a few of the companies that I know write low-cost policies are those listed on the comparison table in Chapter 10, as well as Southwestern, Executive, Old Republic, Old Line, Occidental for a best buy on $250,000 and over, and Guardsman for a good price on hard-to-buy $50,000–$99,999. Unfortunately, all these figures may change tomorrow, so whatever the agency delivers, you will have to check it against the comparison table.

Your local agency can certainly arrange to write you a policy on one of those companies if it does not have a competitive company of its own stuck away in a drawer. Do not feel sorry for the salesman if he complains about the extra work. You have already done a big part of his work when you call him; you've brought him a client.

However and wherever you finally get your lowest rate, you will have to fill out an application. Much of the information required will be obvious (name, age, address, Social Security number), but I can offer some advice on other questions. Most policies have a two-year contestability period, during which the company will not pay if you commit suicide or if you die as a result of something you gave false information about. You can avoid this simply by not killing yourself and not lying.

Except it isn't that simple. If some people told the truth they'd never get an insurance policy. For example, a question on the application asks if you have used marijuana or narcotics within the past ten years. I remember a client, a nice young woman who probably hadn't smoked a half-dozen joints in her life, who put down Yes.

Her application was rejected. Suppose she had instead written No, and been accepted. If she died within two years, the company could refuse to pay the death benefit *only* if using marijuana was the cause of her death.

To illustrate this point further, I'll cite my own case. The question is asked, Have you ever flown as pilot or crew of an airplane, or intend to train for such flying? If the answer is Yes, you've got to fill in an additional questionnaire. Although I've been a private pilot, I have given it up. To avoid the hassle of the aviation questionnaire, I answer No. Only if I die in the crash of a plane I am piloting can the company refuse to pay, and that's not going to happen.

The questionnaire asks if you have used alcoholic beverages within the last ten years. Whether you have a beer a year, or drink like a fish, put down "social drinking only." That's your opinion.

I would not advise listing every cough, dizzy spell, or chest pain—unless you have told your doctor. That puts a different light on everything. All your medical records will be available for scrutiny, now and forevermore. Do not fudge on anything you have ever told any doctor or hospital or have been treated for. It could mean that your survivors will not get the insurance you are paying for.

Unless you read such documents carefully, you do not realize how much privacy you sign away on your insurance application. I always brushed past the authorization paragraph. I was afraid that if people read it they wouldn't sign it. This is what it says—and what you sign.

I hereby authorize any licensed physician, medical practitioner, hospital, clinic or other medical or medically related facility, insurance company, the Medical Information Bureau or other organization, institution or person that has any records of me, my health, or any member of my family, to give to —— COMPANY, or its reinsurers, any such information. I have received the Medical Information Bureau disclosure notice. A Photographic Copy of this authorization shall be as valid as the original.

Note that there is no termination date. This is forever.

I have advised several of my clients in recent years to write in at the end of the paragraph, above the signature, the following: Authorization expires —— (three months from date). This was done with one $500,000 policy and several $100,000 policies, and there were no problems. If it does jeopardize the policy, you can always back down.

When you have signed, the salesman tears off a perforated notice at the bottom of the application and presents it to you. If you read it, you're in for a shock. It says the company may report information about you to the Medical Information Bureau, a national clearing house. And on the back of this tear-off slip is a notice to the effect that information may be obtained on you—"character, reputation, mode of living"—through personal interviews with your neighbors, friends, or acquaintances.

Good-by privacy.

Pumping the neighbors about you can be more damaging than you think. I nearly lost a very big commission when someone told an investigator that my client had two martinis for lunch. I did lose another client because the busybody in the next apartment said he was living with a woman he wasn't married to. It was true, but what did it have to do with insurance? Is everyone living with someone he's not married to uninsurable?

And who judges what? If your next-door neighbors are Moral Majority teetotalers, and look over the back fence and see you pour a thimble of amontillado for your grandmother, will they tell the insurance company gumshoe that you are an alcoholic and give wild parties?

And will he tell your boss?

I'm sorry to say, having called this to your attention, that I can't suggest any action you can take without jeopardizing your insurance.

To return to the application, here are some other suggestions, most of which have been covered in detail elsewhere.

Thanks to the 1981 tax law, most persons worth less than $600,000 can simply name their wife and children or other persons as beneficiaries and let it go at that. If you are leaving your wife more than $600,000, it is true that she can inherit it tax free—but what happens when *she* dies? Unless she has remarried, or spent it, that money is taxable. I recommend setting up a trust, both to own the policy and disburse the funds. Your lawyer can do it for a fee. The trust officer of a bank will do it for nothing.

If no trust is set up, I recommend that you specify under *settlement option* (how the company will pay off when you die) that the money be held by the company at interest subject to withdrawal on demand of the beneficiary. This will prevent the dumping of a large amount of cash on the emotional survivor, and also protect the interests of contingent beneficiaries.

If you have children by another marriage, or other dependents you want to provide for, name them as contingent beneficiaries, or better, set up a trust to provide for everyone. Otherwise, if your wife inherits your estate and she dies without any provision being made, the estate goes to *her* heirs.

If you have any unusual situation, outside the norm of a wife and kids, consult an attorney or trust officer.

How will you pay for this insurance? The salesman will suggest that you pay annually, in advance, or by bank draft (automatic withdrawal from your bank account). Either way he gets his commission immediately. You can also pay semiannually, quarterly, or monthly. I prefer to stretch it out as far as possible, in order to have the use of the money myself, but the nuisance and postage of monthly payments may not be worth it. A monthly bank draft would please everybody.

After you and the salesman have filled out the application, a physical examination may be required. Perhaps you will only be asked for an APS (attending physician's statement). Let's hope you are accepted; your salesman certainly does. But do not get carried away and let him sell you more insurance than you need just because you passed your physical.

If you do *not* pass your physical, two things can happen. You can be rejected, or you can be rated. This means you will have to pay a higher premium. In either case, I suggest that you tell your salesman to explore further. Another advantage in dealing with a general agency is that it can shop around. When I was with Metropolitan I had a client who'd had a heart attack. He even carried nitro in his pocket. He paid a very high rate for his insurance. When I became a general agent representing many companies, I was surprised to find one, Transport Life of Texas, that took him on for half the cost.

Finally, you have your insurance policy. Do not waste it. There is simply no way of knowing how many people die each year without anyone knowing they were insured. The amount could be in the billions. To ensure that your death benefit is paid, therefore, keep records of your policy. Its physical existence is not important; the number *is.* I would keep the policy in a safe place at home and a copy in my safety deposit box, and the name of the company and number of the policy with a copy of my will at the trust office of the bank. If you don't have a will, *make one now,* whether or not you have insurance. Make sure your heirs know about both will and insurance. The company will pay the death benefit, but it has to know you're dead. And it will be very difficult for you to tell them.

This insurance policy is only the beginning. You wouldn't buy a car and expect it to last you the rest of your life, would you? You make periodic checks on your clothes, your TV set, your supply of Jack Daniels—why should insurance be any different? Further, it is one of those rare commodities, like home computers, whose price keeps going down even in a period of inflation. You can keep on firing off your payments unthinkingly, or you can be smart and take advantage of the lower prices.

But it may require some effort. As a licensed broker I received a routine announcement in 1982 of Standard Security's new reduced rates. Shortly after, Cathy received a renewal notice for her $50,000 policy with the same company: $78.50. But if she bought it under the new rates I'd just received, she'd only pay $59. I called the company in New

York. They said the only way she could get the lower rate would be to cancel her current policy and reapply for a new one under the new rates. I told them this procedure would cost the company many times the money involved in administrative expenses. They said, Well, that's the way it is. For two days I talked to nobody but idiots. Finally I reached an intelligent executive who could understand what I was talking about. She authorized the renewal under the new rate, and that was it. We saved twenty bucks.

How much more difficult it would have been if I weren't a broker: we wouldn't even have known of the change in rates. But if it was worth doing for a $50,000 policy that was low-priced to begin with, imagine the savings that could be effected by older people with larger policies by simply running a comparison check each year. That also applies to your home insurance, your car insurance, *all* insurance. Check and see.

Chapter 17

Disability Insurance

Could anything be worse than death? Yes, I think total
disability is worse; it's living death. Life insurance makes it
possible to provide for your dependents after death, but it
doesn't help if you are disabled to the extent that you not
only can't take care of them but they have to take care of you.
Nor is this a remote possibility. Men from ages twenty to
thirty are three times as likely to suffer a prolonged disability
(90 days or more) than death. As you grow older the percentage of longer periods and permanent disability increases.

For this awful possibility I recommend disability insurance. Not accident and health insurance, as sold by mail and
through membership organizations that should know better,
but *disability* insurance. There's a difference.

For medical and hospitalization expenses I recommend
Blue Cross-Blue Shield, basic policy and major medical. As
a nonprofit organization I figure it gives the best deal.

Disability insurance is more complicated. It must be tailored to the individual. A person whose company is going to keep him on the payroll for a definite period can purchase a less expensive plan than someone who is self-employed. And there are many points in between.

Many companies provide disability insurance to their employees at no cost or pay a large percentage of the cost. They think it's good business. They can buy better coverage for a large group at less cost. Donald L. Shepherd, CLU, a New York expert who writes disability insurance for some sixty corporations, said nine out of ten pay the entire cost. One of his corporate clients pays $37,000 a year to cover 400 personnel. Disability payments to most employees run $3,000 a month, less Social Security and workmen's compensation. Top executives receive $6,000 a month. This is the maximum most insurance companies pay; they suspect that for more than that people would stay sick and stay home. The limits on individual policies are much less.

Insurance companies make money on disability insurance. They work on the time value of money. They collect when you are young, and even if they have to give it back to you later, they have had the use of it in the meantime.

The insurance salesman, however, does *not* make money on individual disability policies. The commission is low and the premium is low. It is to the salesman's advantage, therefore, to squeeze every cent out of you for permanent life insurance, for which he gets 55 percent and up.

And further, it's complicated. The most expensive disability policy is *non-cancelable*—only the insured can cancel or change it. The company insures you for the same annual premium, same benefit, until a specified age.

Guaranteed renewable insurance requires the company to renew each year, but the premium may go up.

Cancelable, the least expensive, means that the company can refuse to renew. Companies writing it say they cancel only when they are convinced fraud is involved. I would feel secure with this insurance only if I had an agent with lots of clout handling it for me.

I recommend *Guaranteed renewable.*

That's only the beginning. Rates differ with occupation and income. A major part of the cost of disability insurance is governed by the *elimination period* and the *pay-out period.* If you could start drawing compensation the day you become disabled and continue it until you die the cost would be enormous. If you think your employer and your savings would carry you for an elimination period of six months or a year, you would pay less. If you want the pay-out period to last the rest of your life, you pay more.

With so many variables, quoting rates would be meaningless. I suggest that you estimate the length of your elimination period and the amount of your income should you become disabled. (Do not count on Social Security; it has a five-month elimination period and is tough to get. But you can buy an option for the company to pay you if Social Security doesn't.) Then shop for disability insurance just as you did life insurance.

Before going with an educational institution and its group coverage, I had disability insurance with a small, competitive company, Springfield Life. Other companies that write disability insurance include Mutual of Omaha (the largest), Connecticut General, Continental, Paul Revere, Union Mutual, and Massachusetts Casualty.

Chapter 18

KISS!

If this was a book on how to buy automobiles or stereo equipment I could quit right here—you would know enough to make an informed purchase.

But when it comes to life insurance, intelligent people seem to become helpless pawns. One of my first projects in my new position at the college was to check the alumnae insurance program. Frankly, I was surprised that there was one.

It took me a while to put the story together. One of the dozens of organizations marketing group insurance plans to colleges had contacted the college a year or so before. A representative flew in and not only sold the program but also sold it without anybody realizing that he was a life insurance salesman who'd get a commission on every policy.

He took the list of more than ten thousand alumnae and sent out a solicitation. The women would buy term insurance, and the college would get the dividends as a contribution. But the big deal was that sometime in the future, when the children are grown and the alumnae are wealthy, the alumnae could convert the term insurance to permanent and make the college the beneficiary. Their gift to their alma mater. What a sizzle. More than sixty took out policies.

When all those dividends were supposed to come rolling in, however, they didn't. But still the college authorities were willing to continue with the program. In their naïveté, so typical of people when it comes to insurance matters, they thought they were offering their alumnae a good deal for the present, and the college a good deal for the future. It never occurred to anybody to compare the premiums with other available policies. I find it absolutely amazing that people in America, who know the difference between the price of one bar of soap and another, just simply accept without question the cost of an insurance premium.

A quick look showed that the rates of the term insurance were much higher than average. Rates for women are usually lower. Yet in comparison to the policy I had at the time, in which a male, age thirty-five, paid $117, the policy we were recommending to our alumnae cost $360.

At the age of sixty, my policy would cost $741; the policy we were recommending to our students would cost them $5,371 at age sixty.

We dropped that program like a hot potato, but as far as I know, there are some one hundred other colleges still participating, still recommending that their alumni buy a very high-priced insurance plan.

I have no personal knowledge of this, but *Best's Review,* the leading insurance trade magazine, reported in its November 1980 issue that an aggressive insurance agency attacking permanent insurance was having great success in the South, especially Texas. The agency, A. L. Williams and Associates, based in Atlanta, recruited thousands of salesmen and trained them in a hard-sell program to replace policyholders' permanent plans with a modified premium term policy written by Massachusetts Indemnity and Life.

Best's quoted other insurance agents as saying the new salesmen criticize the insurance industry savagely, apparently using some of the arguments put forward in this book. They convince their prospects that they should replace their whole life policies with term.

And then they sell them a form of deposit term insurance with a high initial premium—and commissions up to 230 percent! All under the guise of consumerism.

The big new policy of 1982, which really does have some innovative features, is generally known as "the universal life policy." The Hartford Life Insurance Company (the one with the deer) sells theirs under the name of The Solution. The Liberty Life Insurance Company calls theirs The Answer. These universal policies were obviously designed by the industry to respond to consumerist criticism—to the FTC's exposé of poor interest rates, for example, and to my recommendation that you buy term insurance and set up your own cash value side fund.

Universal policy salesmen outline a program in which the insurance companies do it all for you—sell you term insurance, set up your side fund earning tax-deferred interest, let you put extra money into it, take it out again, skip payments. They'll even *tell* you, in an annual statement, how much of your money went for insurance, how much into the savings funds.

And the interest rates they advertise—10.5 percent, 12 percent!

I've had people come up and tell me, "Hey, the agent says I'll be getting *twelve* percent!"

And I say, "Great! Twelve percent *of what?*"

It almost hurts to see the expression on their faces as that sinks in. Twelve percent of what, indeed. Of the total amount they put in? Twelve percent of that part of their premium that goes for the death benefit? For the various fees? For the salesman's commission? Of course not. Twelve percent of the cash value. Okay, but how much is the cash value?

Jane Bryant Quinn, *Newsweek*'s financial analyst, looked at several universal policies on the basis of the $1,000 premium a forty-year-old man would pay for a $100,000 policy. One company would take $902 for fees and insurance, another the whole thing, and another, which did have some left over, paid only 4 percent on the first $1,000.

Universal insurance is too complicated, like most gimmicks the industry's marketing people dream up, to analyze simply. But let me ask you a question: When you deposit a thousand bucks in the savings bank, does the teller slip 55 percent or more of it into her purse?

My answer to universal life insurance is the same as that for any other high-cost insurance plan. Don't buy it.

The product developers and marketers in the insurance industry are so greedy and clever that they continually strive to stay ahead of those few of us who advise the consumer intelligently and honestly. You can bet that as soon as this book and its message begin to be talked about, the boys in the three-piece suits are going to design new plans that appear to jump on my bandwagon. And your local salesmen, armed with new gimmicks and sales manuals, are going to make their pitch.

I wish I could sit down with you personally and help you analyze every insurance program somebody tries to sell you. Instead, I will give you a magic formula. It has been proven effective, millions of times, all over the country.

It is what the life insurance industry gives its salesmen to use against you, the consumer. Now I am giving it to you to use to your advantage against them.

The magic charm is
K I S S
It stands for
Keep It Simple, Stupid

As a young salesman I was taught, and as a manager I taught my salesmen, how to use the magic formula.

Insurance is so complicated that to explain it adequately is over everybody's head, including the salesman's. So, the industry says, don't try. Tell only as much as you need to tell to make the sale. Don't go into things the customer doesn't ask about. Don't tell—*sell.* Keep it simple, stupid.

KISS!

Here's how you, consumer, can use the magic formula. Remember, the salesman is taught to *give* only as much information as is necessary to make the *sale.*

So you turn the tables. *Get* only as much information as you need to make the *purchase.*

You need only two things.

First, ask if the policy is *renewable.* That's all, just that one word, renewable. If it is not renewable do not buy it at any price.

Second, ask the salesman to give you in writing the total amount you will have to pay for your insurance per year. That means what it says: What is the total amount you will have to write a check for, what is the total amount that will be deducted from your bank account?

You are not interested in complications—dividends he says you are going to get back, deposits you are only going to make once. All you want to know from him is: *How much do I have to give you the first year?* (And you can say under your breath, *Keep it simple, stupid.*)

On receiving the total amount in writing, compare it with the table in Chapter 10. It will either be a good buy or a bad buy. Buy it or don't buy it. In either case you have used the industry's own magic formula to your own advantage. KISS!

It does not matter what the insurance you buy is called, or who it is you buy it from. My message to you in this book is: Buy the lowest-priced insurance to provide your survivors with money if you should die. Put all or a portion of what you save into an investment program to build up your fortune whether you die or live. Either way, you win. I hope you live and enjoy every penny of it.

Appendix

Mr. Term and Mr. Perm, Participating

Chapter 14 contained figures and tables showing that permanent insurance, non-participating, provides less and costs more. This appendix will repeat the exercise for participating policies. For it I selected policies from the Consumers Union report on life insurance. In permanent insurance, participating, CU rated Teachers' Insurance and Annuity Association number one. As that is not available to the public, I chose number two, the Home Life Insurance Company's non-smoker whole life policy. I telephoned the home office and asked for a ledger statement for a twenty-five-year-old male, $100,000 life insurance. The ledger statement arrived promptly, giving me all the figures I had requested for the first twenty years of the policy, and for ages sixty and sixty-five. It took me weeks to get the pertinent figures for the policy years from twenty-one to forty, ages forty-six to sixty-five.

Obtaining the net premiums for term insurance was even

more difficult. Again I chose the annual renewable term policy rated second only to TIAA. It happened to be the Metropolitan Life Insurance Company's policy. Again I was able to get the figures for the first twenty years quite easily, but not the advanced years. At one time I had three different sets of figures for the second twenty years. Finally I hounded the people at my former office into getting me a computer printout of the accurate figures.

The ledger statements for both policies list the annual premiums, then the estimated dividend paid at the end of the year. As there is no dividend the first year, this in effect means that the dividend does not really affect the premium until the third year.

And the dividend may not affect the premium at all. It may not be paid. Both policies pointed out that the figures given for dividends are not guarantees or even estimates. The salesman will gloss over this, of course, but nevertheless the disclaimer is printed there, plain as day, on the ledger statement.

As these are the figures that the companies furnish, these are the figures I have to use. In the table in Chapter 14, you recall, I gave the premium for permanent insurance, the premium for term insurance, and the difference between the two. We will follow the same procedure here, with the extra specification that the premiums are *net* premiums. This means that I have deducted the appropriate dividend from the annual premium. Once again, we have no way of knowing that the dividends will actually be paid.

If you look at the table, "Mr. Perm versus Mr. Term, Par," you will see that there are some striking differences in the premiums. The annual premium for the permanent policy decreases until, after thirty years, Mr. Perm is no longer paying the company. Rather, the company is paying him. Mr. Term's dividends also reduce his net premium, but never to the point where he is collecting instead of paying.

After we deduct the unguaranteed, unestimated figures

MR. PERM VERSUS MR. TERM, PAR

1 AGE	2 YEAR	3 P	4 T	5 P−T	6 SF	7 CV	8 DB(P)	9 DB(T)
25	1	$1,051	$209	$842	$926	$0	$100,000	$100,926
26	2	947	210	737	1,830	0	100,000	101,830
27	3	946	145	801	2,894	100	100,000	102,894
28	4	942	147	795	4,057	1,100	100,000	104,057
29	5	919	149	770	5,310	2,100	100,000	105,310
30	6	888	153	735	6,650	3,100	100,000	106,650
35	11	693	170	523	14,876	8,700	100,000	114,876
40	16	483	214	269	26,525	15,400	100,000	126,525
45	21	307	317	−10	43,507	22,800	100,000	143,507
50	26	130	555	−425	68,607	30,700	100,000	168,607
55	31	−70	914	−984	106,727	38,700	100,000	206,727
60	36	−271	1,573	−1,844	162,274	46,800	100,000	262,274
64	40	−439	2,355	−2,794	225,385	53,500	100,000	325,385

EXPLANATION OF COLUMNS
1. Age of insured
2. Policy year
3. Net premium for permanent (P) policy (estimated dividends have been deducted)
4. Net premium for term (T) policy (estimated dividends have been deducted)
5. Net permanent premium less net term premium
6. Side fund: difference invested at 10%
7. Cash value of permanent policy
8. Death benefit, permanent policy
9. Death benefit, term plus side fund.

and enter the resulting net premiums in Columns 3 and 4, the rest of the exercise is the same as the non-par table in Chapter 14. As you see, at the age of thirty, Mr. Perm has the same death benefit, $100,000, that he has had and will have all along, while Mr. Term has built up a side fund of $6,650 to add to his face value of $100,000. Even at the age of sixty-four, when Mr. Term's premium is $2,794 more than Mr. Perm, he will still have nearly a quarter of a million dollars in his side fund.

As in Chapter 14, the corresponding table which follows shows the tremendous impact of the time value of money in death benefits.

To determine how much it actually cost Mr. Perm and Mr. Term for their insurance if they die at any given year, again we follow the formula as explained in the non-par chapter.

Table 1 and Table 2 concern the death benefits of the two

TABLE 1
**WHAT WILL MY FAMILY RECEIVE
IF I DIE?**

Age	Mr. Perm	Mr. Term
30	$100,000	$106,650
35	100,000	114,876
40	100,000	126,525
45	100,000	143,507
50	100,000	168,607
55	100,000	206,727
60	100,000	262,274
64	100,000	325,385

TABLE 2
**WHAT DID THE INSURANCE
REALLY COST ME UPON DEATH?**

Age	Mr. Perm	Mr. Term
30	$8,115	$1,465
35	18,334	3,458
40	33,381	6,856
45	56,331	12,824
50	92,133	23,526
55	149,136	42,409
60	238,964	76,690
64	347,969	122,584

insured. Is not the death benefit, the money your survivors get when you die, the reason you take out insurance? If not, it should be. However, as millions of people have bought permanent insurance because some salesman told them it was a good investment, I will go on to show what each plan will provide in case Mr. Perm and Mr. Term decide to get out of their respective programs.

Table 3, which follows, shows the side fund built up by Mr. Term in comparison to the cash value in Mr. Perm's policy. In order to get that cash value, of course, Mr. Perm has to cash in his policy and give up the rest of his insurance, or borrow it at the rate of interest the company specifies.

TABLE 3
WHAT WILL I RECEIVE IF I QUIT?

Age	Mr. Perm	Mr. Term
30	$3,100	$6,650
35	8,700	14,876
40	15,400	26,525
45	22,800	43,507
50	30,700	68,607
55	38,700	106,727
60	46,800	162,274
64	53,500	225,385

Table 4 shows what it has actually cost Mr. Perm and Mr. Term to have the amount shown above, i.e., total premium compounded at 10 percent less money returned as cash value or side fund.

TABLE 4
WHAT DID THE INSURANCE
REALLY COST ME WHEN I QUIT?

Age	Mr. Perm	Mr. Term
30	$5,015	$1,465
35	9,634	3,458
40	17,981	6,856
45	33,531	12,824
50	61,433	23,526
55	110,436	42,409
60	192,164	76,690
64	294,469	122,584

ABOUT THE AUTHOR

WALTER S. KENTON, JR., is a graduate of the
American College of Life Underwriters, a Chartered Life Underwriter and a member of the Million-Dollar Round Table. After seventeen years
with the insurance industry as salesman, sales
manager, general agent and broker, he retired in
1980 in order to write this book. He is currently
Director of Estate Planning for a small prestigious
college in Virginia.